WORLD W

WORLD WAR II KILLED MORE PEOPLE AND COST MORE MONEY THAN ANY OTHER WAR IN HISTORY. IT WAS FOUGHT IN THE SKIES, ON THE SEAS, ON THE GROUND, AND UNDERGROUND. MORE THAN FIFTY NATIONS TOOK PART.

NO OTHER WAR WAS EVER SO DESTRUCTIVE. SOME 60 MILLION PEOPLE WERE KILLED. MORE THAN ONE-THIRD OF THEM WERE NOT EVEN IN THE ARMED FORCES.

IT WAS A WAR OF DEATH CAMPS AND BOMBED CITIES, OF GREAT HEROISM AND GREAT HORROR. IT WAS ALSO A WAR FOR SURVIVAL, AS THE ALLIES STRUGGLED TO KEEP THE AXIS FROM CONQUERING THEM AND THE WORLD.

BLITZKRIEG

At dawn on September 1st, 1939, nine armoured Nazi columns moved across the eastern borders of Germany into Poland. They hurried across the flat Polish plains.

In a few hours, the invaders had ridden deep into Poland.

Meanwhile, the main Nazi infantry marched across the border to join the advance force.

The mobile troops sped towards key defence targets, capturing or destroying bridges, railway junctions and airfields.

OVERHEAD, BOMBERS OF THE NAZI AIR FORCE, THE LUFTWAFFE, SWOOPED DOWN ON POLISH AIRFIELDS. NEARLY ALL POLISH PLANES WERE DESTROYED ON THE GROUND.

OTHER NAZI PLANES BOMBED POLISH CITIES AND MACHINE GUNNED REFUGEES WHO BEGAN FLEEING FROM THE INVADERS.

IN THE FIRST FEW DAYS, THERE WERE NO MAJOR CLASHES. THE POLISH ARMY RETREATED EASTWARD.
WE ARE NO MATCH FOR THE NAZI TANKS AND PLANES!

BY SEPTEMBER 10TH, THE ADVANCE-GUARD NAZIS REACHED THE OUTSKIRTS OF WARSAW, THE POLISH CAPITAL. THERE, THE POLES HAD DUG TRENCHES FOR A LAST-DITCH DEFENCE.
WE CAN HOLD THE GERMANS HERE.

Seven days later, the defenders of Warsaw learned of a new attack.

"The Russian army has just crossed our eastern border! Now defeat is only a matter of time."

Within two days, the Russians overran the eastern half of Poland. On September 27th, the last of the Warsaw defenders surrendered to the Nazis.

"Warsaw is ours. This is a memorable day for us."

In twenty-seven days, the Nazis, with the help of Russia, had crushed Poland. This was lightning war, or Blitzkrieg, a type of warfare the Nazis would use many times in Europe.

Hours after the German invasion began, the British demanded the Nazis withdraw their forces from Poland. The Nazis ignored this demand. On September 3rd, 1939, Great Britain and France declared war on Nazi Germany. World War II, the greatest armed struggle in history, had begun.

4

THE FUEHRER

THE GERMANY THAT OVERRAN POLAND WAS RULED BY A DICTATOR NAMED ADOLF HITLER. HITLER'S RISE TO POWER BEGAN IN THE DAYS FOLLOWING WORLD WAR I.

IN 1919, GERMANY WAS A DEFEATED NATION. SHE HAD LOST WORLD WAR I, AND HER ECONOMY WAS WEAKENED. HER GOVERNMENT, CALLED THE WEIMAR REPUBLIC, WAS DISLIKED BY MANY GERMANS.

THE REPUBLIC CAN DO NOTHING FOR GERMANY.

IF YOU REALLY BELIEVE THAT, YOU SHOULD JOIN OUR NEW PARTY, THE NATIONAL SOCIALISTS.

THE NATIONAL SOCIALISTS, OR NAZIS, WANTED TO OVERTHROW THE WEIMAR REPUBLIC. IN 1920, IN MUNICH, ADOLF HITLER BECAME ONE OF THE NAZIS' LEADING SPOKESMEN.

WE MUST RESTORE GERMANY TO HER RIGHTFUL PLACE AS LEADER OF THE WORLD!

THREE YEARS LATER, HITLER PROCLAIMED HIMSELF DICTATOR OF THE GERMAN STATE OF BAVARIA. BUT WHEN HE ATTEMPTED A REVOLUTION, HE WAS ARRESTED BY THE WEIMAR REPUBLIC.

YOU HAVE BEEN FOUND GUILTY OF TREASON AND ARE HEREBY SENTENCED TO FOUR YEARS IN PRISON.

HITLER'S SENTENCE WAS LATER REDUCED TO THIRTEEN MONTHS. IN PRISON, HE OUTLINED HIS PHILOSOPHY IN HIS BOOK, MEIN KAMPF.*

EXPANSION IS THE KEY TO GERMANY'S FUTURE.

*MY STRUGGLE

IN 1929, THE GERMAN ECONOMY WAS SHATTERED IN A WORLD-WIDE DEPRESSION. HITLER BUILT UP HIS FORCES, CALLED STORM TROOPS. HE WON THE SUPPORT OF MANY ARMY LEADERS AND INDUSTRIALISTS. HIS SPEECHES ALSO WON OVER THE GERMAN PEOPLE.	BY 1932, THE NAZI PARTY WAS THE LARGEST IN THE GERMAN PARLIAMENT. A YEAR LATER, THE REPUBLIC'S PRESIDENT NAMED HITLER CHANCELLOR, OR PRIME MINISTER.

"THERE ARE GREAT DAYS AHEAD FOR GERMANY."

"NOW I SHALL LEAD AS I HAVE PROMISED."

THE NAZI GOVERNMENT WAS CALLED THE THIRD REICH. THE NAZIS BANNED ALL BOOKS THAT DID NOT AGREE WITH THEIR IDEAS. IN 1933, BERLIN STUDENTS, LED BY NAZI PROPAGANDA MINISTER PAUL JOSEPH GOEBBELS, BURNED THOUSANDS OF BOOKS IN EVENING TORCHLIGHT RALLIES.	GOEBBELS SET UP STRICT STANDARDS FOR GERMAN TEACHERS.

"ALL GERMAN CHILDREN BELONG TO THE THIRD REICH. TEACHERS MUST FOLLOW THE TEACHINGS OF THE STATE."

Newspaper editors who disagreed with the Nazis were imprisoned or shot.

"You have written an editorial criticising the state's handling of schools. You are under arrest! Your newspaper shall be shut down."

In 1934, the president of Germany died, and Hitler proclaimed himself Fuehrer*.

"I swear to give my unconditional obedience to Adolf Hitler, Fuehrer of the Third Reich."

*LEADER

As dictator, Hitler outlawed all other political parties. He built up the German army in violation of the World War I peace treaty*. In 1936, he sent troops into the Rhineland, a district of Germany bordering France, again violating the treaty.

*THE TREATY OF VERSAILLES

Then, in 1938, he met with the Chancellor of Austria.

"You have treated the German people in Austria poorly. Now your hour has come!"

7

On March 11th, 1938, the Nazis took over Austria. There was no resistance.

Hitler assured the world that he was only invading Austria to preserve the independence of the Germans living there.

"This is the end of our territorial claims in Europe."

But six months later...

"The Germans in Czechoslovakia must be protected. It is our duty to take over the Sudetenland*."

*The western part of Czechoslovakia

Hitler's plans worried other major European powers. On September 30th, 1938, the prime ministers of Great Britain and France met with Hitler in Munich, Germany.

"I assure you that this is the last territorial demand I shall make in Europe."

They agreed to Hitler's demands, and on October 1st, the Nazis marched into the Sudetenland. Then, on March 15th, 1939, they took over the rest of Czechoslovakia.

Many world leaders were alarmed. Among them was Winston Churchill.

This is only the foretaste of a bitter cup which will be proffered to us year by year unless we take our stand for freedom as in the olden time.

But Hitler did not intend to be stopped. On May 22nd, he signed a mutual-aid treaty with Benito Mussolini, dictator of Italy. On August 23rd, Germany and the Soviet Union signed a pact in which each pledged not to attack the other.

The Russians have agreed not to stop us from invading Poland, so long as they gain territory, too.

Thus, the stage was set for the Nazi invasion of Poland and the beginning of World War II. By late 1939, the Nazis had almost doubled the land area of Germany.

WAR ON THE HIGH SEAS

In the first two months of the war, Nazi submarines, or U-boats, sank sixty-seven Allied ships. Great Britain's first major naval loss occurred on October 14th, 1939. The Nazi submarine U-47 entered the well-protected British naval base at Scapa Flow, Scotland, and sank the battleship Royal Oak with six torpedoes. The submarine avoided the tight British defences and escaped into the Atlantic.

The Nazi battleship Graf Spee sank many Allied merchant ships in the South Atlantic. On December 13th, 1939, she was attacked by three British cruisers. Badly damaged, the Graf Spee pulled into Montevideo Harbour, Uruguay, for repairs. The Uruguayan government ordered her to leave immediately. Rather than see her sunk by the British, Hitler ordered her captain to scuttle her. On December 20th, the Graf Spee was blown up by the Germans.

IL DUCE

Like Hitler, Italian dictator Benito Mussolini believed in armed might and expansion through conquest. The partnership of Hitler's Germany and Mussolini's Italy was called the Rome-Berlin Axis.

In 1919, many Italians were dissatisfied with the peace terms of World War I.

"We helped win the war but we gained none of the rewards!"

That same year, Mussolini took advantage of the people's unrest and organised a political group called Fascists.

"I promise you that Italy will again know the glory that was once Rome's!"

In 1923, the Fascists overthrew the Italian government, and Mussolini became dictator. At first, he put through many reforms which improved Italy's economy.

"Under Il Duce*, there are more jobs. He even makes the trains run on time."

But the depression of 1929 hit Italy hard, and the people began to question the Fascist leadership. Mussolini turned to thoughts of conquest.

"Italy must move onward with strength. The world will soon respect our bayonets!"

*THE LEADER

IN 1934, ITALIAN TROOPS IN AFRICA CLASHED WITH SOME ETHIOPIANS. EMPEROR HAILE SELASSIE OF ETHIOPIA CALLED THE ITALIANS AGGRESSORS. MUSSOLINI, WANTING WAR, BLAMED ETHIOPIA.
UNLESS WE RECEIVE AN APOLOGY, OUR ARMIES WILL TAKE ACTION!
THE MATTER WAS TAKEN UP BY THE LEAGUE OF NATIONS, AN INTERNATIONAL ORGANISATION SET UP AFTER WORLD WAR I. BUT THE LEAGUE WAS POWERLESS. ON OCTOBER 3RD, 1935, 250,000 ITALIAN TROOPS INVADED ETHIOPIA.
THE ETHIOPIAN DEFENCE, 35,000 POORLY ARMED SOLDIERS FELL BEFORE THE MECHANISED ITALIAN FORCES.
ON MAY 5TH, 1936, ETHIOPIA WAS MADE A PART OF ITALIAN EAST AFRICA. HAILE SELASSIE WENT TO GENEVA, SWITZERLAND TO APPEAL TO THE LEAGUE OF NATIONS. HIS SPEECH SYMBOLISED THE DANGERS THREATENING THE WORLD.
IT IS A QUESTION OF THE VALUE OF PROMISES MADE TO SMALL STATES THAT THEIR INDEPENDENCE SHALL BE RESPECTED. APART FROM THE KINGDOM OF GOD, THERE IS NOT ON THIS EARTH ANY NATION THAT IS HIGHER THAN ANY OTHER.

THE CONQUEST OF WESTERN EUROPE

In the spring of 1940, the key word was supply. If the Nazis were to beat Britain and France they would need new sources of raw materials – especially iron. With this in mind, Hitler scanned the map of Europe and moved north.

On April 9th, 1940, Nazi troops overran Denmark in twenty-four hours.

On the same day, the Nazis invaded Norway. In twelve hours, parachute troops captured nearly every major military post.

In mid-April, a British force captured Narvik, Norway's northernmost port, but had to withdraw two months later. Another British force landed in central Norway, but was almost wiped out in four days by the Nazis.

By taking Norway, Hitler gained a string of vital air bases and tons of Norwegian ores.

On May 10th, the Nazi blitzkrieg thundered into Holland. The Dutch army fought valiantly but was hopelessly outnumbered.

The Dutch declared Rotterdam an open city*. But on May 14th, the Nazis bombed the city, killing more than thirty thousand civilians and levelling hundreds of buildings.

*A city where all defences have been abandoned

Holland surrendered in five days. Belgium, which was also invaded on May 10th, surrendered in less than three weeks. A large British force in Belgium, along with many French, Belgian and Polish troops, retreated to Dunkirk, a port on the northeast coast of France.

The German army headed towards Dunkirk to trap the retreating Allied forces.

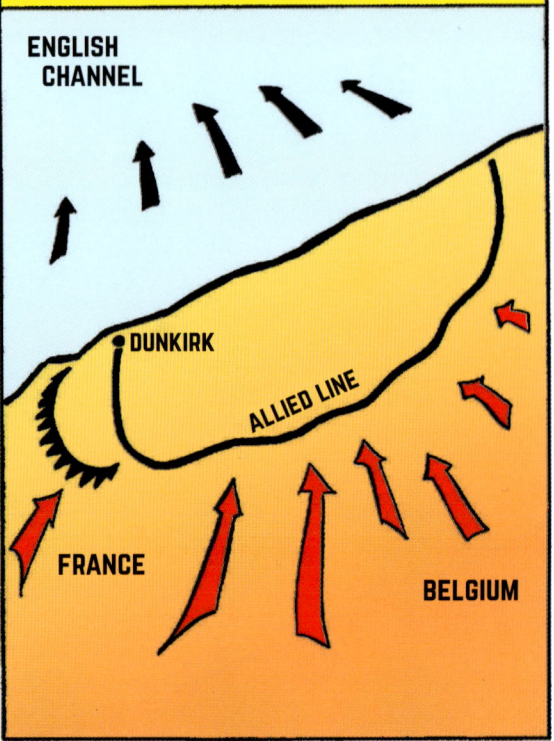

ENGLISH CHANNEL

DUNKIRK

ALLIED LINE

FRANCE

BELGIUM

On May 26th, the Nazis were certain they would win a great victory.

The British and French armies are cut off at Dunkirk. Complete surrender is only hours away.

But a rescue armada was formed out of British naval vessels, private yachts, fishing schooners, cargo ships and even tugs pulling barges.

She's not very big, but she can cross the channel and pick up a platoon or two.

Altogether, 887 ships and boats sped towards Dunkirk from England. The vessels dodged Nazi bombs to pick up the retreating armies.

MANY OF THE BRITISH BOATS WERE MANNED BY CIVILIANS.
STEP LIVELY! WE'LL GET YOU OUT OF HERE!
OVERHEAD, PLANES OF THE BRITISH ROYAL AIR FORCE DROVE OFF MANY OF THE NAZI BOMBERS.
A SMALL FORCE OF BRITISH AND FRENCH TROOPS FOUGHT A REAR-GUARD ACTION TO PREVENT THE NAZIS FROM REACHING THE COAST.
THE RESCUE OPERATIONS LASTED NINE DAYS AND SAVED 338,226 MEN. A CRUSHING DEFEAT WAS TURNED INTO A MORAL VICTORY.
I CAN'T BELIEVE IT! THEY GOT US BACK TO ENGLAND!

MEANWHILE, THE NAZIS MARSHALLED THEIR FORCES FOR AN ALL-OUT ATTACK ON FRANCE. IN THE EARLY DAYS OF THE WAR, BOTH THE NAZIS AND FRENCH DID LITTLE FIGHTING. THE FRENCH COUNTED ON THEIR MAGINOT LINE, A GREAT SYSTEM OF FORTIFICATIONS FACING GERMANY, TO PROTECT THEM.

THE GERMANS STAYED BEHIND THEIR SIEGFRIED LINE, A STRING OF FORTS FACING THE MAGINOT LINE.

THE LACK OF FIGHTING CAUSED MANY PEOPLE TO CALL THE STALEMATE A "PHONEY WAR". THEN, ON JUNE 6TH, 1940...

TODAY, ONE HUNDRED GERMAN DIVISIONS MOVE TO CRUSH FRANCE.

THE NAZIS TORE THROUGH THE FRENCH DEFENCES. FRENCH TROOPS RETREATED TO THE SOUTH AND WEST.

MUSSOLINI DECIDED TO SHARE THE NAZI VICTORY. WHEN HE WAS SURE FRANCE WAS BEATEN, HE SENT FOUR HUNDRED THOUSAND ITALIAN TROOPS INTO THE FRENCH RIVIERA.

PARIS FELL TO THE NAZIS ON JUNE 14TH.

THE FRENCH GOVERNMENT FLED PARIS SOUTH TO TOURS. THERE, FRENCH PREMIER PAUL REYNAUD APPEALED TO THE UNITED STATES FOR AID.

SEND US CLOUDS OF AEROPLANES AND WE WILL HURL BACK THE INVADERS.

BUT FRANCE WAS DOOMED. REYNAUD WAS REPLACED BY MARSHAL HENRI PÉTAIN. ON JUNE 17TH, THE FRENCH PEOPLE HEARD PÉTAIN ASK FOR A SURRENDER.

IT IS FUTILE TO CONTINUE THE STRUGGLE AGAINST AN ENEMY SUPERIOR IN NUMBERS AND ARMS. IT IS WITH A HEAVY HEART THAT I SAY WE MUST CEASE THE FIGHT.

Four days later, Hitler and his deputies arrived in Compiègne, near Paris, to receive the French surrender. The meeting took place in the same railway car in which the Germans had surrendered at the end of World War I!

On September 3rd, 1939, England and France declared war on Germany without any basis. Now, France has been conquered.

The terms were hard. The Nazis would occupy more than half of France, with the French paying the cost of occupation. Unoccupied France would be headed by a government friendly to the Nazis*.

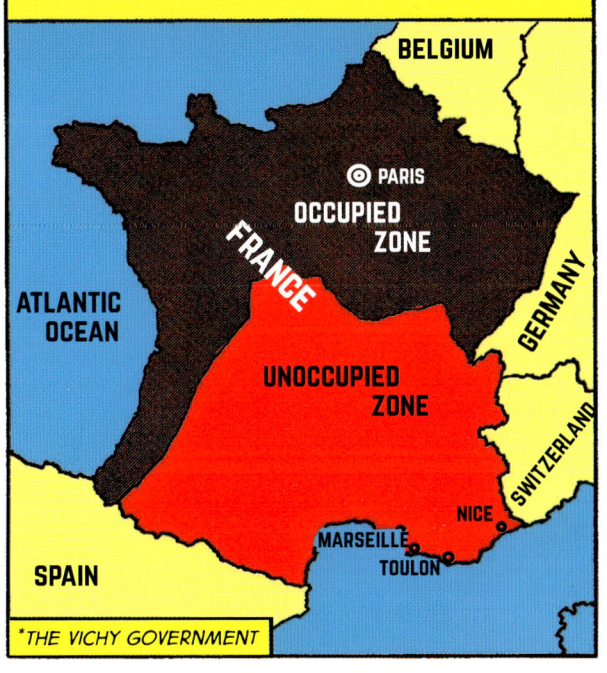

*The Vichy Government

The terms also stated that all French warships would be turned over to the Nazis. On July 3rd, off Oran, Algeria, the British Navy destroyed three French battleships and two destroyers to prevent them from falling into Axis hands.

Many French soldiers escaped to North Africa and England. In London, General Charles de Gaulle took command of the Free French Army.

We will continue the fight. France has lost a battle, but France has not lost the war.

THE BATTLE OF BRITAIN

After the fall of France, Britain stood alone, the only power preventing Nazi Germany from gaining complete mastery of Western Europe.

The British spirit was symbolised in the speeches of Winston Churchill, who became Prime Minister on May 10th, 1940.

"Hitler knows that he will have to break us in this island or lose the war. Let us therefore so bear ourselves that, if the British Empire last for a thousand years, men will still say, 'This was their finest hour.'"

On August 6th, more than one thousand Nazi bombers struck English factories, airfields and cities. R.A.F. fighter planes, often outnumbered, rose to meet the bombers.

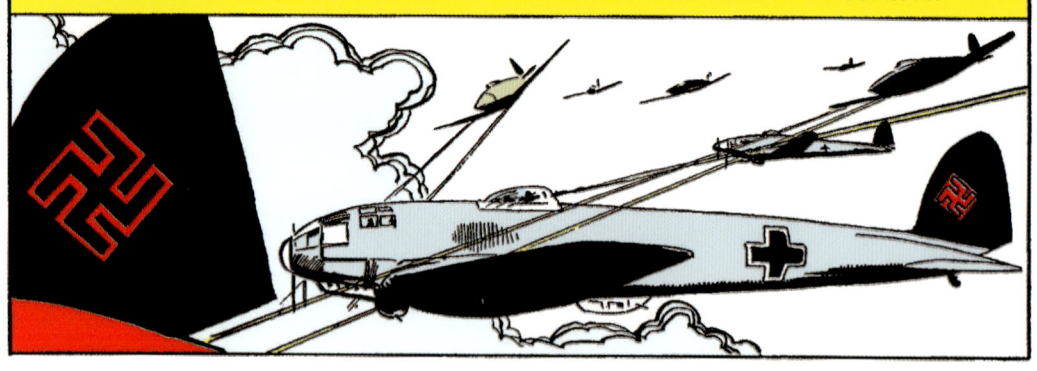

The R.A.F. inflicted heavy losses on the Nazi planes.

"The gratitude of every home goes out to the British airmen. Never in the field of human conflict was so much owed by so many to so few."

The British resistance infuriated Hitler. On September 7th, he unleashed his bombers on London. Londoners went into air-raid shelters.

More than eight hundred Nazi planes bombed the city, killing 430 people and starting more than one thousand fires.

The air attacks on London continued for several months.

On November 14th and 15th, a huge Nazi bomber force hit Coventry, England, levelling the entire centre of the city and killing or wounding more than one thousand people.

Meanwhile, Hitler prepared for an invasion of England. German soldiers practiced landing exercises on the shores of France and Belgium.

HITLER HAD HOPED TO SOFTEN UP ENGLAND THROUGH HIS AIR STRIKES. BUT THE BRITISH RESISTED SO STRONGLY THAT, ON OCTOBER 21ST, HE CANCELLED HIS INVASION PLANS.
WE WILL WAIT UNTIL NEXT SPRING, WHEN WE HAVE THE WHOLE SUMMER AHEAD OF US.
NORD SEE

THE INVASION NEVER CAME. BRITAIN WORKED TO BUILD UP ITS MILITARY STRENGTH. SOME AID CAME FROM THE UNITED STATES.
THE YANKS HAVE GIVEN US FIFTY DESTROYERS IN RETURN FOR LETTING THEM USE OUR NORTH AMERICAN BASES.

THE BRITISH BOUGHT MUCH OF THEIR MILITARY GOODS FROM THE UNITED STATES, BUT THEIR GOLD WAS RUNNING OUT. THEN, LATE IN 1940, PRESIDENT FRANKLIN D. ROOSEVELT BROADCAST AN IMPORTANT MESSAGE.
LET US SAY TO THE DEMOCRACIES: WE SHALL SEND YOU, IN EVER INCREASING NUMBERS, SHIPS, PLANES, TANKS, GUNS. THIS IS OUR PURPOSE AND OUR PLEDGE.

THE RESULT WAS THE LEND-LEASE PROGRAM. IN MARCH 1941, THE UNITED STATES AUTHORISED 7 BILLION DOLLARS IN AID TO BRITAIN. THREE MONTHS LATER, ROOSEVELT AND CHURCHILL MET AND DREW UP THE ATLANTIC CHARTER. THE DOCUMENT SPOKE OUT FOR FREEDOM AND AGAINST THE NAZI TYRANNY.

WARSHIPS AND WOLF PACKS

IN MAY 1941, THE NAZIS READIED FOR ACTION THEIR GREATEST WARSHIP, THE BISMARCK. ON MAY 24TH, SHE SANK THE BRITISH CRUISER HOOD IN THE NORTH ATLANTIC. THE BRITISH FLEET TRACKED HER DOWN TWO DAYS LATER, SOUTH OF IRELAND. AFTER BEING BADLY DAMAGED BY TORPEDO PLANES, THE BISMARCK WAS SUNK ON MAY 27TH BY SEVERAL BRITISH SHIPS.

IN 1940, THE ALLIES SET UP A CONVOY SYSTEM IN WHICH MERCHANT SHIPS WERE PROTECTED FROM GERMAN U-BOAT ATTACKS BY WARSHIPS. TO COUNTER THIS, NAZI GRAND ADMIRAL KARL DOENITZ ORDERED HIS U-BOATS TO TRAVEL TOGETHER IN WOLF PACKS. IN THE FIRST SIX MONTHS OF 1942, WOLF PACKS SANK 585 ALLIED SHIPS. BY MID-1943, SUPERIOR ALLIED NAVAL POWER ENDED THE U-BOAT MENACE.

THE RESISTANCE

When the Nazis occupied the countries they conquered, they soon found themselves plagued by a new enemy – the fighters of the Resistance, or Underground. These were civilians who braved torture and death to help free their homelands by destroying Nazi fortifications and factories. They fought in every occupied country.

In Copenhagen, Denmark, the sabotage was conducted by two groups, the BOPA, short for Borgerlige Partisaner, or Civil Partisans, and the Holger Danske*. Late in the war, the BOPA called a special meeting.

"The Globus factory is making parts for Nazi rockets."

"The buildings are well guarded, but we should try to blow them up."

*Named after a mythical Danish hero

After three months of planning, the BOPA went into action. One group, dressed as road workers, began tearing up the highway between the factory and a nearby German military post.

The men dug trenches in which they buried electrically wired charges. Then they covered up the road.

"If the Germans try to come at us from this side of the factory, we can blow up the road behind us."

A few days later, more than one hundred BOPA members assembled near the factory. Some of them looked like campers, but their knapsacks contained guns, grenades and explosives.

THE GROUP SPLIT UP AND CREPT INTO THE GARDENS OF NEARBY HOUSES. AT EXACTLY 7PM, THEY RACED TO THE BARBED-WIRE FENCES SURROUNDING THE FACTORY. THEIR GRENADES AND GUNFIRE KILLED SEVERAL NAZI GUARDS.

SOME BOPA MEMBERS RUSHED THROUGH THE MAIN GATES, PROTECTED BY FIRE FROM THE MEN SURROUNDING THE FACTORY.

WHILE PART OF THE GROUP STOOD GUARD, A DEMOLITION CREW PLANTED SEVERAL EXPLOSIVE CHARGES IN STRATEGIC AREAS OF THE PLANT.

THE BOPA GROUP THEN RACED FROM THE FACTORY TO TWO BUSES WAITING ON THE HIGHWAY. THE BUSES SPED AWAY.

WHEN THE EXPLOSIONS RIPPED THE FACTORY APART, THE GROUP WAS SEVERAL HUNDRED FEET DOWN THE HIGHWAY. THE BUSES WERE FIRED AT BY NAZI GUARDS AT ANOTHER FACTORY ON THE ROAD, BUT ONLY ONE MAN WAS KILLED. THIS ACTION, THE FIRST MAJOR DAYLIGHT SABOTAGE ATTACK IN DENMARK, HELPED HALT NAZI ROCKET PRODUCTION AND EARNED THE BOPA THE RADIOED CONGRATULATIONS OF THE ALLIED HIGH COMMAND.

THE EASTERN FRONT

Late in 1940, Hitler and Mussolini turned their attention to the Balkan Peninsula. Of the eight countries on or near the peninsula, three – Hungary, Romania and Bulgaria – joined the Axis powers. Turkey remained neutral. Italy had taken over Albania in 1939.

HUNGARY
YUGOSLAVIA
ROMANIA
ALBANIA
BULGARIA
GREECE
TURKEY

■ PRO-AXIS GOVERNMENTS

In early October, 1940, Nazi troops moved through Hungary and Romania.

Mussolini was eager to prove the might of his Italian troops. On October 28th, two hundred thousand Italian troops invaded Greece. The Italians were confident of an easy victory.

"THE GREEKS WILL FLEE BEFORE OUR TANKS AND ARTILLERY."

The Greek infantry waited in the hills until the Italians were far from their supply bases. Then they struck.

"THE GREEKS ARE EVERYWHERE! OUR MEN ARE FLEEING!"

Panel 1	Panel 2

Panel 1 (narration): THE ITALIANS SUFFERED ONE DEFEAT AFTER ANOTHER IN GREECE. THEY RETREATED TO ALBANIA. MUSSOLINI REFUSED TO ADMIT HIS FORCES WERE BEATEN.

- HITLER WANTS TO KNOW IF WE NEED HELP.
- WE'LL BREAK THE BACKS OF THE GREEKS, AND WE DON'T NEED ANY HELP!

Panel 2 (narration): HITLER DID NOT AGREE. ON APRIL 6TH, 1941, HIS FORCES INVADED YUGOSLAVIA AND GREECE. YUGOSLAVIA FELL IN ELEVEN DAYS, GREECE IN TWENTY-FIVE.

Panel 3 (narration): MOST OF THE BRITISH TROOPS THAT HAD BEEN FIGHTING WITH THE GREEKS RETREATED TO THE ISLAND OF CRETE IN THE MEDITERRANEAN SEA. ON MAY 20TH, THE NAZIS INVADED CRETE.

Panel 4 (narration): IN LESS THAN TWO WEEKS, THE NAZIS CONQUERED THE ISLAND. SEVERAL THOUSAND BRITISH TROOPS WERE EVACUATED IN DESTROYERS TO EGYPT.

WITH THE FALL OF THE BALKANS, HITLER WAS MASTER OF EUROPE. HE HAD SIGNED A PACT WITH RUSSIA IN 1939. BUT ON JUNE 21ST, 1941, HE WROTE TO MUSSOLINI. *THERE IS EVIDENT IN RUSSIA A CONSISTENT TREND TO EXPANSION. I HAVE DECIDED TO CUT THE NOOSE BEFORE IT CAN BE DRAWN TIGHT.*	**T**HE NEXT DAY, 135 NAZI DIVISIONS INVADED THE SOVIET UNION. WHILE NAZI PLANES DESTROYED MUCH OF THE SOVIET AIR FORCE ON THE GROUND, NAZI ARMOURED TROOPS SURGED INTO SOVIET TERRITORY.
THE FIRST NAZI THRUSTS EXTENDED FOUR HUNDRED MILES. THE NAZIS WERE ONLY TWO HUNDRED MILES FROM MOSCOW. HITLER'S GENERALS URGED AN ALL-OUT ATTACK ON THE RUSSIAN CAPITAL, BUT THE FUEHRER HAD OTHER PLANS. *WE WILL STRIKE AT LENINGRAD, MOSCOW, KIEV AND ODESSA AT THE SAME TIME.*	**K**IEV AND ODESSA WERE TAKEN. OTHER GERMAN FORCES NEARED MOSCOW AND LENINGRAD.

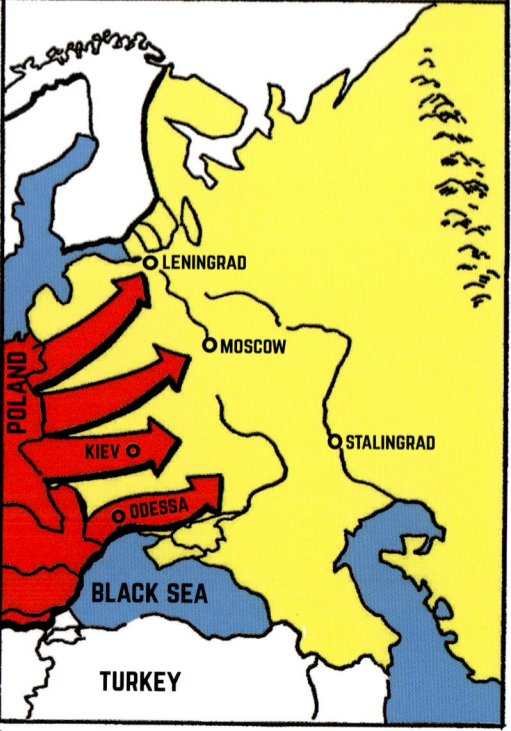

IN NOVEMBER, COLD WEATHER BEGAN TO HALT THE NAZI OFFENSIVE. HITLER'S GENERALS WANTED TO CALL OFF THE ATTACK ON MOSCOW UNTIL THE SPRING.
WE MUST NOT WAIT. ONE GREAT THRUST NOW AND MOSCOW IS OURS!
THE NAZIS REACHED THE MOSCOW SUBURBS ON DECEMBER 2ND, BUT THE RUSSIAN WINTER WAS AN UNCONQUERABLE ENEMY.
THE ENGINES OF OUR TANKS ARE FROZEN. OUR MEN HAVE NO WARM CLOTHING. INFORM BERLIN OUR SITUATION IS DESPERATE.
SOVIET FORCES COUNTERATTACKED, CAPTURING MANY TANKS AND WEAKENING NAZI SUPPLY ROUTES.
MEANWHILE, NAZI FORCES BESIEGED LENINGRAD. THEY HOPED TO CHOKE OFF THE LIFE OF THE CITY BY CUTTING OFF ITS PORT, HIGHWAYS, RAILROADS AND CANALS.

But the people of Leningrad refused to yield. They brought in munitions and food across their only connection with the rest of Russia – the frozen waters of Lake Ladoga.

Slowed by the winter, the Nazis retreated at all points in Russia. In some areas, they lost two hundred miles of territory.

The Nazi invasion brought the Soviet Union into the Allied camp.

"BRITAIN AND THE UNITED STATES WILL SEND RUSSIA AS MUCH AID AS POSSIBLE."

While the Nazi armies floundered in the Russian snows during the winter of 1941, a new enemy on the other side of the world was preparing to attack...

THE BIG THREE

THE FORTY-SEVEN COUNTRIES THAT EVENTUALLY DECLARED WAR ON ONE OR MORE OF THE AXIS POWERS WERE CALLED THE ALLIES. THE MOST IMPORTANT OF THE ALLIES WERE GREAT BRITAIN, THE BRITISH COMMONWEALTH COUNTIES, THE UNITED STATES AND RUSSIA.

WINSTON CHURCHILL

AS GREAT BRITAIN'S PRIME MINISTER, CHURCHILL WORKED DIRECTLY WITH MILITARY LEADERS IN FORMING BRITISH WAR POLICY. HIS SPEECHES, DETERMINATION AND FAMED V-FOR VICTORY SALUTE RALLIED THE SPIRITS AND THE FORCES OF THE BRITISH COMMONWEALTH AND THE FREE WORLD.

FRANKLIN D. ROOSEVELT

AS PRESIDENT OF THE UNITED STATES BEFORE AND AFTER HER ENTRY INTO THE WAR, ROOSEVELT PREPARED THE NATION FOR THE COMING CONFLICT BY INCREASING THE SIZE OF THE ARMED FORCES. HE STRONGLY SUPPORTED THE ALLIES FROM THE ONSET. ON AUGUST 12TH, 1941, HE AND CHURCHILL JOINTLY ISSUED THE ATLANTIC CHARTER. THEY PLEDGED TO RESPECT THE RIGHT OF EVERY PEOPLE TO CHOOSE ITS OWN FORM OF GOVERNMENT. THE CHARTER LAID DOWN SOME OF THE PRINCIPLES OF WORLD POLITICS FOR WHICH THE ALLIED NATIONS WERE FIGHTING.

JOSEPH STALIN

STALIN FIRST ARRANGED A PACT FOR RUSSIA WITH THE NAZIS TO PRESERVE PEACE BETWEEN THE TWO NATIONS AND TO DIVIDE POLAND AFTER CONQUERING IT. ALTHOUGH STALIN WAS WARNED OF HITLER'S INTENTION TO INVADE RUSSIA, HE MISJUDGED THE NAZI THREAT. THE RUSSIAN ARMY WAS TAKEN BY SURPRISE WHEN THE NAZIS MARCHED IN. STALIN DECLARED HIMSELF MARSHAL OF ALL SOVIET FORCES IN THE RUSSIAN COUNTER-OFFENSIVE.

WAR IN THE PACIFIC

In the late 1920s, many Japanese military leaders were dissatisfied with their country's role in the world.

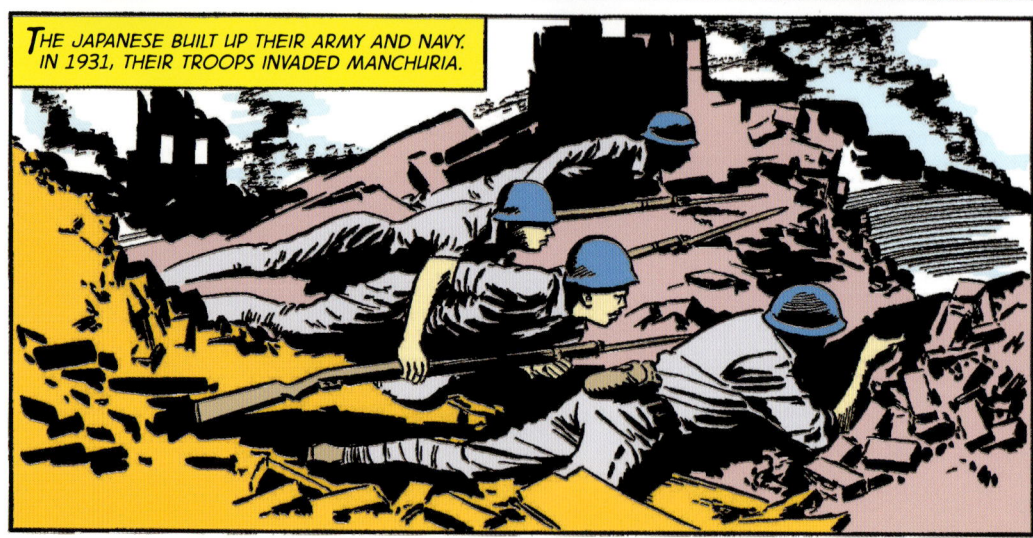

"Japan needs room to expand. Our islands are too small for our growing population."

The Japanese built up their army and navy. In 1931, their troops invaded Manchuria.

China, which controlled Manchuria, appealed to the League of Nations. The League could do nothing to help. By 1932, Japan had overrun Manchuria.

"We are now on the doorstep of China."

In the next four years, Japanese militarists came into power. They assassinated political leaders and industrial chiefs who opposed their plans of conquest for Japan.

IN JULY 1937, THE JAPANESE INVADED CHINA. THE FIGHTING WAS BITTER.

JAPAN WAS CAREFUL NOT TO DISTURB BRITISH OR AMERICAN INTERESTS. IN SEPTEMBER, HOWEVER, JAPANESE PLANES BOMBED A UNITED STATES GUNBOAT IN CHINA.

IN NEED OF AMERICAN IRON AND STEEL, THE JAPANESE APOLOGISED. BUT IN 1938, THE UNITED STATES TOOK ECONOMIC STEPS AGAINST THE JAPANESE WAR MACHINE.

THE UNITED STATES HAS HALTED SALES OF AIRCRAFT TO JAPAN.

IN 1940, THE UNITED STATES, BRITAIN AND THE NETHERLANDS REDUCED THEIR EXPORTS TO JAPAN. IN TOKYO, THE MILITARISTS JOINED THE GERMAN-ITALIAN AXIS AND MADE GENERAL HIDEKI TOJO THE JAPANESE PREMIER.

THE UNITED STATES MUST GIVE US A FREE HAND IN CHINA AND ALLOW US TO TAKE THE DUTCH EAST INDIES.

THE UNITED STATES DEMANDED THAT THE JAPANESE LEAVE CHINA AND WITHDRAW FROM THE AXIS. THE JAPANESE REFUSED. THEN, ON DECEMBER 7TH, 1941, THE JAPANESE ATTACKED HICKAM FIELD, THE AMERICAN AIRBASE IN HAWAII.

THE CARRIER-BASED JAPANESE BOMBERS CAUGHT THE AMERICANS BY SURPRISE. DOZENS OF AMERICAN PLANES WERE DESTROYED ON THE GROUND.

THE MAIN OBJECTIVE OF THE ATTACK WAS THE AMERICAN PACIFIC FLEET AT PEARL HARBOUR, HAWAII. MORE THAN ONE HUNDRED JAPANESE PLANES SWOOPED DOWN ON THE SEVENTY AMERICAN COMBAT SHIPS LYING PEACEFULLY IN THE HARBOUR.

THE BATTLESHIP OKLAHOMA SANK IN TEN MINUTES. THE ARIZONA ALSO SANK, AND SIX OTHER BATTLESHIPS WERE BADLY DAMAGED. HALF OF THE AMERICAN NAVY WAS CRIPPLED IN THE ATTACK.

THE NEXT MORNING, PRESIDENT ROOSEVELT ASKED THE UNITED STATES CONGRESS TO DECLARE WAR ON JAPAN.

YESTERDAY, DECEMBER 7TH, 1941 – A DATE WHICH WILL LIVE IN INFAMY – THE UNITED STATES OF AMERICA WAS SUDDENLY AND DELIBERATELY ATTACKED BY NAVAL AND AIR FORCES OF THE EMPIRE OF JAPAN.

BOTH THE UNITED STATES AND BRITAIN DECLARED WAR ON JAPAN ON DECEMBER 8TH. THREE DAYS LATER, GERMANY AND ITALY DECLARED WAR ON THE UNITED STATES. IN THE PACIFIC, THE JAPANESE INVADED THE AMERICAN POSSESSIONS OF GUAM AND WAKE ISLANDS. GUAM SURRENDERED QUICKLY.

ON WAKE, THE FIRST JAPANESE LANDING WAS BEATEN OFF. MAJOR JAMES DEVEREUX COMMANDED THE SMALL UNITED STATES MARINE DETACHMENT ON THE ISLAND.

HERE'S A RADIO MESSAGE FROM THE NAVY DEPARTMENT, SIR. THEY ASK IF WE NEED ANYTHING.

YOU CAN TELL THEM TO SEND US MORE JAPS!

BUT THE WAKE FORCE SURRENDERED ON DECEMBER 23RD. MEANWHILE, OTHER JAPANESE TROOPS INVADED THE BRITISH POSSESSIONS OF HONG KONG AND MALAYA. HONG KONG SURRENDERED ON CHRISTMAS DAY.

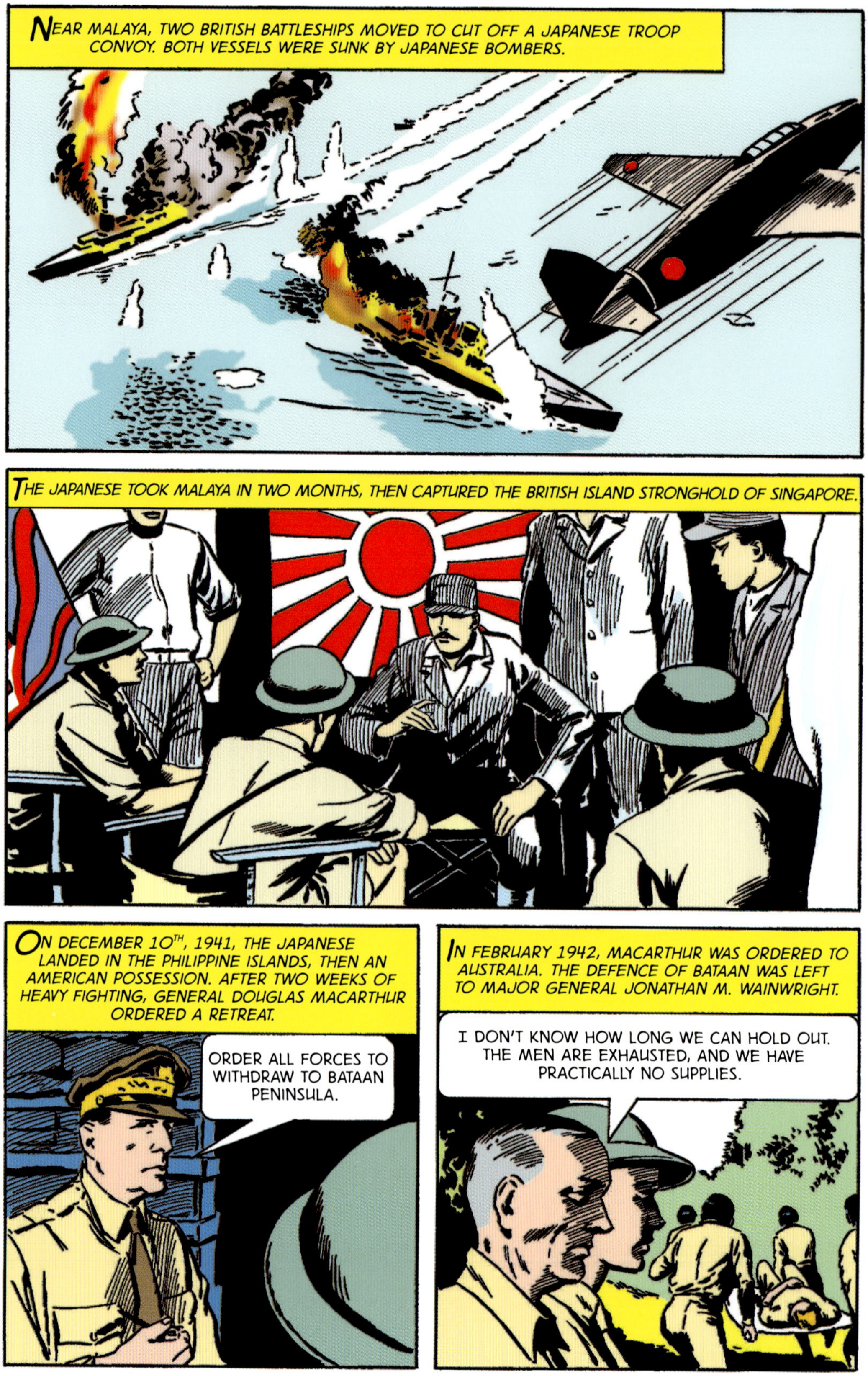
NEAR MALAYA, TWO BRITISH BATTLESHIPS MOVED TO CUT OFF A JAPANESE TROOP CONVOY. BOTH VESSELS WERE SUNK BY JAPANESE BOMBERS.
THE JAPANESE TOOK MALAYA IN TWO MONTHS, THEN CAPTURED THE BRITISH ISLAND STRONGHOLD OF SINGAPORE.
ON DECEMBER 10TH, 1941, THE JAPANESE LANDED IN THE PHILIPPINE ISLANDS, THEN AN AMERICAN POSSESSION. AFTER TWO WEEKS OF HEAVY FIGHTING, GENERAL DOUGLAS MACARTHUR ORDERED A RETREAT.
ORDER ALL FORCES TO WITHDRAW TO BATAAN PENINSULA.
IN FEBRUARY 1942, MACARTHUR WAS ORDERED TO AUSTRALIA. THE DEFENCE OF BATAAN WAS LEFT TO MAJOR GENERAL JONATHAN M. WAINWRIGHT.
I DON'T KNOW HOW LONG WE CAN HOLD OUT. THE MEN ARE EXHAUSTED, AND WE HAVE PRACTICALLY NO SUPPLIES.

BATAAN SURRENDERED ON APRIL 9TH. THIRTY-FIVE THOUSAND AMERICAN AND FILIPINO TROOPS WERE FORCED TO MARCH EIGHTY-FIVE MILES TO A JAPANESE PRISON. MANY OF THE PRISONERS DIED OF BEATINGS AND STARVATION.

WAINWRIGHT AND ELEVEN THOUSAND AMERICAN TROOPS RETREATED FROM BATAAN TO THE ISLAND OF CORREGIDOR FOR A LAST-DITCH STAND. THE ISLAND FORTRESS SUFFERED A CONSTANT BOMBARDMENT.

ON MAY 6TH, WAINWRIGHT SURRENDERED TO THE JAPANESE.

OTHER JAPANESE FORCES INVADED INDO-CHINA, BURMA AND THE DUTCH EAST INDIES. BY THE SUMMER OF 1942, JAPAN CONTROLLED A LARGE PORTION OF THE SOUTHWEST PACIFIC AND THREATENED AUSTRALIA.

ALEUTIAN
CHINA
JAPAN
MIDWAY
WAKE IS.
PHILIPPINES
NEW GUINEA
AUSTRALIA ■ CONTROLLED BY JAPAN

THE DOOLITTLE RAID

After the attack on Pearl Harbour, American forces were on the defensive. Then, early in 1942, Lieutenant Colonel James H. Doolittle presented a plan to top-level American military leaders.

"I believe that a squadron of carrier-based planes could bomb Tokyo. It would be a tremendous blow to Japanese morale."

The plan was approved. Doolittle called for volunteers to man the planes.

"I can't reveal our objective. I can only say that the mission will be extremely dangerous."

Doolittle soon had more than enough volunteers. The men boarded the aircraft carrier "Hornet".

"These aren't carrier planes, they're land bombers - B-25s!"

"They're the only planes we've got with the speed and fuel capacity to reach Tokyo."

The fliers were schooled in special navigation. They made hundreds of practice take-offs.

"We've been training for three months. I think we're ready."

DOOLITTLE PLANNED TO TAKE OFF FOUR HUNDRED MILES FROM JAPAN. BUT EIGHT HUNDRED MILES OUT, THE HORNET CAME UPON A SMALL JAPANESE SHIP AND SANK HER.

THE JAPANESE SHIP MAY HAVE RADIOED OUR LOCATION TO TOKYO. WE'LL TAKE OFF IN THE MORNING.

AT 8:20AM, APRIL 18TH, ALL SIXTEEN B-25s MANAGED THE DIFFICULT TAKE-OFF. THEY FLEW CLOSE TO THE WATER TO ESCAPE JAPANESE RADAR.

THE PLANES TOOK THE JAPANESE BY SURPRISE. BOMBS FELL ON TOKYO, OSAKA, KOBE AND NAGOYA AND DESTROYED SEVERAL FACTORIES AND DOCKYARDS. ONE ROUND HIT A CRUISER UNDER CONSTRUCTION.

THE PLANES FLEW ON OVER CHINA. MOST OF THE AIRMEN BAILED OUT AND MADE THEIR WAY TO ALLIED LINES. SEVEN FLIERS DROPPED IN JAPANESE-HELD TERRITORY AND WERE CAPTURED. THE BOMBING GREATLY BOOSTED ALLIED MORALE AND SHOOK THE JAPANESE. THEY HAD THOUGHT THEIR HOME ISLANDS WERE SAFE FROM ATTACK.

THE CORAL SEA AND MIDWAY

In early May, 1942, a Japanese naval force steamed towards south-eastern New Guinea for an invasion of Port Moresby. In the Coral Sea, the fleet was intercepted by planes from American aircraft carriers. The American planes sank one Japanese carrier, four cruisers and two destroyers. Japanese aircraft sank an American carrier, a destroyer and a tanker. The Japanese fleet turned back and called off the invasion. This was the first naval battle in history in which opposing ships never fired at each other.

The next month, the Japanese planned to invade Midway Island, a United States possession in the central Pacific, only a thousand miles from Hawaii. Heavily outnumbered, the United States Pacific Fleet under Admiral Chester Nimitz met the enemy west of Midway. In the action that followed, the Japanese lost four carriers and 322 planes. One American carrier, a destroyer and 147 planes were downed by the Japanese. The invasion of Midway was called off, and the Japanese expansion to the east was ended. The Battle of Midway was the first major Allied victory in the Pacific. It broke Japan's naval air power.

GUADALCANAL

In June 1942, after their defeat off Midway, the Japanese turned southward. They held two islands in the Solomon Island group. They also occupied the northern half of New Guinea. If they could take the Solomons and all of New Guinea they could launch attacks against Australia.

Early in July, the Japanese moved into Guadalcanal, the key island in the Solomons, and built an airstrip. One month later, American marines landed and took over the strip.

From the strip, the Americans set out to take over the entire island. Much of the fighting took place in dense jungle.

The Japanese proved excellent jungle fighters. Snipers, hidden in the tops of palm trees, caused many American casualties.

THE AMERICANS WERE ALSO PLAGUED BY MOSQUITOES, WHICH CAUSED THOUSANDS OF CASES OF MALARIA.

FOR SIX MONTHS THE BATTLE RAGED, WITH THE AMERICANS SLOWLY PUSHING THE JAPANESE BACK. BY FEBRUARY 1943, MOST OF THE JAPANESE WERE WIPED OUT, AND THE AMERICANS TOOK CONTROL OF GUADALCANAL.

MEANWHILE, IN LATE JULY, 1942, THE JAPANESE IN NORTHERN NEW GUINEA MOVED SOUTH TO ATTACK THE CITY OF PORT MORESBY. AN AUSTRALIAN BATTALION STUBBORNLY DELAYED THE ATTACKERS, BUT THE JAPANESE AT LAST PUSHED THROUGH.

IN LATE AUGUST, TWO THOUSAND JAPANESE LANDED ON THE SOUTHERN TIP OF NEW GUINEA. THE AUSTRALIANS WIPED THEM OUT.

From then on, the Japanese were on the defensive in the South Pacific. In late 1942, an American force landed and pushed the Japanese off southern New Guinea.

In March 1943, the Japanese sent a convoy with twenty thousand troops to reinforce northern New Guinea. American army planes sighted the convoy and sank most of the twenty-two ships.

In late 1943, Australian troops fought up the eastern coast and took over the northeast section of the island.

Then, in April 1944, American forces hemmed in fifty thousand Japanese near Wewak, in north-western New Guinea. In June, New Guinea was firmly in Allied hands.

TARAWA

From the Solomons and New Guinea, Allied forces took New Britain and the Admiralty Islands. The next objective was the Gilbert Islands group, with its key base, Tarawa.

In November 1943, American planes and ships bombarded Tarawa heavily. The three thousand Japanese defenders were protected by underground bunkers with concrete walls five feet thick.

American Marines waded ashore on November 21st. They moved through blistering Japanese fire to attack the bunkers.

After four days of fighting, the remaining Japanese left their bunkers and formed a suicide charge. More than three thousand Americans were killed before the last of the Japanese were wiped out.

Tarawa proved that superior American war production was giving Allied forces an edge in weapons and supplies. It also proved that the Japanese would defend their islands to the last man.

WAR LEADERS

DOUGLAS MACARTHUR

WHEN GENERAL MACARTHUR WAS ORDERED TO LEAVE BATAAN IN 1942, HE ISSUED HIS FAMOUS PROMISE, "I SHALL RETURN." AS COMMANDER OF ALLIED FORCES IN THE SOUTHWEST PACIFIC, HE LED THE INVASIONS OF JAPANESE STRONGHOLDS AND KEPT HIS PROMISE BY LIBERATING THE PHILIPPINES IN 1944.

ISOROKU YAMAMOTO

ADMIRAL YAMAMOTO PLANNED THE ATTACK ON PEARL HARBOUR AND LATER BECAME COMMANDER-IN-CHIEF OF THE JAPANESE COMBINED FLEET. HE LED NAVAL FORCES IN THE BATTLES OF THE CORAL SEA AND MIDWAY. IN APRIL 1943, HE WAS KILLED WHEN AMERICAN FLIERS SHOT DOWN A PLANE CARRYING HIM ON A TOUR OF JAPANESE BASES.

WILLIAM F. HALSEY

ADMIRAL HALSEY LED THE FIRST AMERICAN NAVAL ATTACKS ON THE JAPANESE IN RAIDS ON THE GILBERT AND MARSHALL ISLANDS IN JANUARY, 1942. HE BECAME COMMANDER OF AMERICAN SOUTHWEST PACIFIC NAVAL FORCES LATER IN THE YEAR. HIS CARRIER PLANES AND SHIPS SUPPORTED MANY ALLIED INVASIONS OF JAPANESE-HELD ISLANDS.

STALINGRAD

As the tide began to turn for the Allies in the Pacific, the war in Europe also reached a climax.

Hitler had invaded Russia along a broad front in the summer of 1941. In the north, his troops surrounded Leningrad. In the south, they pushed east towards the oil-rich region of the Caucasus.

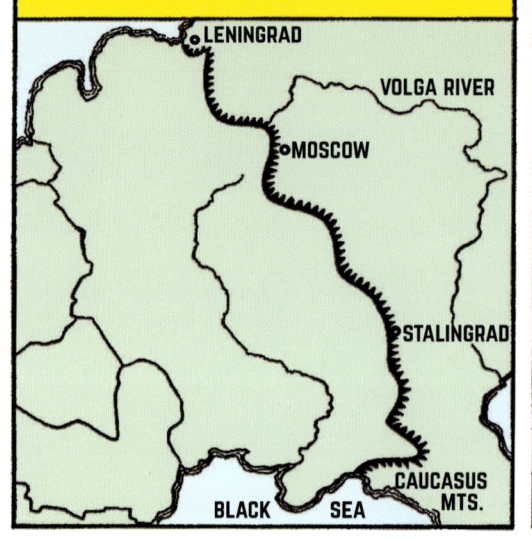

Hitler had expected the conquest of Russia to take a short time. But the German invaders were poorly equipped to withstand the harsh Russian winter of 1941-1942. Russian soldiers forced the enemy back along the frozen battle front.

In spite of heavy losses, Hitler thought he could win victory in 1942. Nearly all Nazi generals felt that Germany lacked the men and arms to conquer Russia.

"We need more tanks and guns."

"Don't tell me what we need! We will march straight to the Volga!"

In the north, the Russians still kept the Germans out of Leningrad. In the south, the Nazi Sixth Army, under General Friedrich von Paulus, reached Stalingrad on the Volga River in late August of 1942.

"Order the artillery to commence fire."

THE BIG GUNS OF THE NAZIS DESTROYED THREE-QUARTERS OF THE CITY IN A SINGLE DAY. THEN THE TANKS MOVED IN.	MANY OF THE TANKS, STALLED BY THE RUBBLE IN THE STREETS, WERE DESTROYED BY RUSSIAN TROOPS THROWING HAND GRENADES.
THE 330,000 NAZI TROOPS FOUND THEIR FIERCEST RESISTANCE OF THE WAR IN THE CITY. BATTALIONS FOUGHT TO TAKE A SINGLE BLOCK. THERE WAS MUCH HAND-TO-HAND FIGHTING.	IN BERLIN, NAZI GENERALS ARGUED THAT THE SIXTH ARMY WAS BEING BEATEN. LET US RETREAT AND REGROUP OUR DIVISIONS BEFORE ANOTHER WINTER SETS IN. NEVER! WE WILL STAY AND FIGHT!

On November 19th, Russian General Georgi Zhukov launched a counterattack.

We will send forces to the north and south of the Nazis and seal them in.

While the Russians moved to encircle the Nazis, the first winter storm struck, paralysing Von Paulus's planes and tanks.

We cannot defeat the Russian winter! Curse the Fuehrer for making us attack!

The Russian ring closed in, pushing twenty-two Nazi divisions into a small pocket. White-clad Russian ski troops descended on Nazi tanks.

The Nazi supply lines were cut. The soldiers ate horses, dogs and cats.

In Berlin, Hitler still refused to accept defeat.

The Sixth Army will not be withdrawn! It will stay where it is!

THE NAZIS HELD ON, HOPING FOR SUPPLIES FROM THE AIR, BUT THEY NEVER APPEARED. THE RUSSIANS DEMANDED IMMEDIATE SURRENDER.

I MUST FOLLOW THE FUEHRER'S ORDERS. WE WILL CONTINUE TO HOLD OUR DEFENCES.

DAY BY DAY, THE RUSSIANS CLOSED THE POCKET. MANY NAZIS SURRENDERED, REDUCING THE SIXTH ARMY TO LESS THAN EIGHTY THOUSAND MEN.

BY LATE JANUARY, 1943, THE NAZI FORCE WAS PRACTICALLY WIPED OUT. ON JANUARY 31ST, VON PAULUS SENT A LAST RADIO MESSAGE TO BERLIN.

TELL THEM WE HAVE HELD OUR POSITION TO THE LAST MAN.

BUT THE MESSAGE WAS FALSE. HOURS LATER, VON PAULUS SURRENDERED. IN TWO DAYS, THE RUSSIANS COMPLETELY CONTROLLED THE AREA. NEARLY TWO HUNDRED THOUSAND NAZIS WERE KILLED OR DIED IN RUSSIAN CAPTIVITY. THE SIEGE OF LENINGRAD WAS NOT BROKEN BY THE RUSSIANS UNTIL JANUARY OF 1944, BUT STALINGRAD WAS THE TURNING POINT. IT COST HITLER ALL CHANCE OF VICTORY IN THE EAST.

WAR LEADERS

ALAN BROOKE
AFTER LEADING ALLIED TROOPS IN THE RETREAT AT DUNKIRK, SIR ALAN BROOKE BECAME COMMANDER-IN-CHIEF OF THE BRITISH HOME FORCES. HE WAS A MAJOR FIGURE IN PLANNING ALL BRITISH OFFENSIVES.

KARL DOENITZ
AS HEAD OF THE NAZI SUBMARINE SERVICE, DOENITZ MADE THE U-BOAT ONE OF THE KEY INSTRUMENTS OF WAR. IN 1943, HE WAS NAMED COMMANDER-IN-CHIEF OF THE NAZI FLEET WITH THE TITLE OF GRAND ADMIRAL.

GEORGI ZHUKOV
AS CHIEF OF STAFF OF THE SOVIET ARMY, MARSHAL ZHUKOV LED THE DEFENCE OF MOSCOW AND THE VICTORY AT STALINGRAD. LATER, HE COMMANDED THE RUSSIAN FORCES WHICH DROVE THROUGH POLAND AND INTO GERMANY.

LIDICE AND WARSAW

In May 1942, Czech patriots killed a Nazi commander. In return, the Nazis machine-gunned all 190 men of the Czech village of Lidice. The women of the town were sent to concentration camps, compounds in which political prisoners of war were confined. There, they were forced to work for the Nazi war effort or were killed. The children were sent to German institutions. Lidice was then set afire and ploughed under to remove every trace of civilisation.

When the Nazis moved into Warsaw, the capital of Poland, four hundred thousand Jews were thrown into the city's ghetto, an old walled-off section. Most of the Jews died of disease and starvation, or were killed by the Nazis. In 1943, only sixty thousand survived. The Nazis sent in the Gestapo* and army troops to capture them, but the Jews resisted fiercely. After four weeks of fighting in the streets and sewers, the Nazis overran the ghetto. More than fifty-six thousand Jews were killed.

*The German Secret Police

THE DEATH CAMPS

In the conquered countries of Europe, as well as in Germany, the Nazis murdered millions of people and displaced millions more from their homes.

While building up the Nazi party in Germany, Hitler constantly preached against certain minority groups.

We must have a pure Fatherland, without the evil influence of the Catholics and Jews!

In the mid-1930s, many Catholic leaders were imprisoned or killed by the Gestapo.

Some Protestant ministers spoke out against Hitler. Among them was Martin Niemoeller.

No more are we ready to keep silent at man's behest when God commands us to speak. For we must obey God rather than man.

In 1937, the Nazis arrested Niemoeller, along with eight hundred of his followers. He was thrown in a concentration camp and stayed there until the end of the war.

THE NAZIS WERE DETERMINED TO WIPE OUT THE ENTIRE JEWISH AND GYPSY POPULATIONS. BEGINNING IN THE LATE THIRTIES, NAZI STORM TROOPERS DESTROYED HUNDREDS OF SYNAGOGUES AND THOUSANDS OF SHOPS OWNED BY PEOPLE OF THE JEWISH FAITH.
AFTER THE WAR BEGAN, THE NAZIS ROUNDED UP ALL THE JEWS IN AN OCCUPIED AREA AND SENT THEM TO DETENTION CAMPS. FROM THERE, HUNDREDS OF THOUSANDS OF PEOPLE WERE HERDED INTO RAILROAD BOX CARS.
EXCUSE ME, DO YOU KNOW WHERE WE ARE GOING?
I DON'T KNOW. THEY GOT US IN THE MIDDLE OF THE NIGHT, AND WE WERE SENT DIRECTLY HERE.
THEY WERE BROUGHT TO A LARGE AREA SURROUNDED BY AN ELECTRICALLY CHARGED BARBED-WIRE FENCE. AT THE GATE, A GUARD SEPARATED THEM INTO TWO GROUPS.
ALL MEN OVER FORTY-FIVE, ALL MOTHERS AND ALL CHILDREN UNDER FOURTEEN ON THIS SIDE.
AUSCHWITZ
THE PEOPLE ON ONE SIDE HAD NO IDEA THAT THEY WOULD NEVER SEE THE OTHERS AGAIN. ALL THOSE WHOM THE NAZIS CONSIDERED TO BE UNFIT FOR LABOUR WERE SENT INTO A LARGE, ROUND BUILDING.
IT IS ONLY A SHOWER ROOM. LEAVE YOUR CLOTHES IN THE ROOM OUTSIDE.
A FEW MOMENTS LATER, A POISON GAS WAS SPRAYED INTO THE CHAMBER. WITHIN HALF AN HOUR, EVERYONE INSIDE WAS DEAD.
THIS NEW CHEMICAL WORKS WELL, HERR KOMMANDANT. WE CAN KILL 3,000 OF THEM AT A TIME.

AFTER GOLD FILLINGS AND WEDDING RINGS WERE REMOVED FROM THE BODIES, THEY WERE BURNED. FOR THOSE WHO WERE SPARED THE GAS CHAMBER, DEATH TOOK DIFFERENT FORMS. PRISONERS WERE CROWDED TOGETHER AND GIVEN LITTLE FOOD AND NO MEDICAL CARE.

WHEN I WOKE UP THIS MORNING I FOUND HERMANN'S BODY ON THE BENCH NEXT TO ME. HE DIED DURING THE NIGHT.

THE HARDY ONES WHO DID NOT DIE OF DISEASE DIED OF STARVATION. WITH ONLY SMALL FOOD ALLOWANCES, THE PRISONERS WERE MADE TO WORK FROM SUNRISE TO SUNSET AT BACKBREAKING LABOUR.

THE NAZIS BEGAN TO USE PRISONERS FOR HIDEOUS OPERATIONS AND EXPERIMENTS. THEY KEPT SOME MEN OUT OF DOORS IN TANKS OF SEA WATER IN THE WINTER, TO SEE HOW LONG THEY WOULD SURVIVE.

KILL ME, PLEASE!

IN ALL, THE GERMANS SLAUGHTERED MORE THAN SEVEN MILLION PERSONS IN CONCENTRATION CAMPS. WHEN THE ALLIES LIBERATED THE CAMPS, THE MOUNDS OF DEAD BODIES WHICH THE NAZIS, IN THEIR HASTE, HAD NOT HAD TIME TO BURN, STOOD SILENT WITNESS TO WHAT HAD PASSED.

OH, MY GOD!

NORTH AFRICA

In 1942, Africa was divided up among many nations. After Italy declared war on Britain on June 10th, 1940, she began to build up military strength in her African colonies. She hoped to take over Egypt and the Sudan, then British colonies. This would close off Britain's oil supply, which came through the Suez Canal.

The French colonies in Africa were controlled by the Vichy government of unoccupied France, which was a puppet of the Nazis. Italy and Germany together prevented any Allied shipping from entering the Mediterranean Sea, and all supplies to Egypt had to come by way of the Cape of Good Hope.

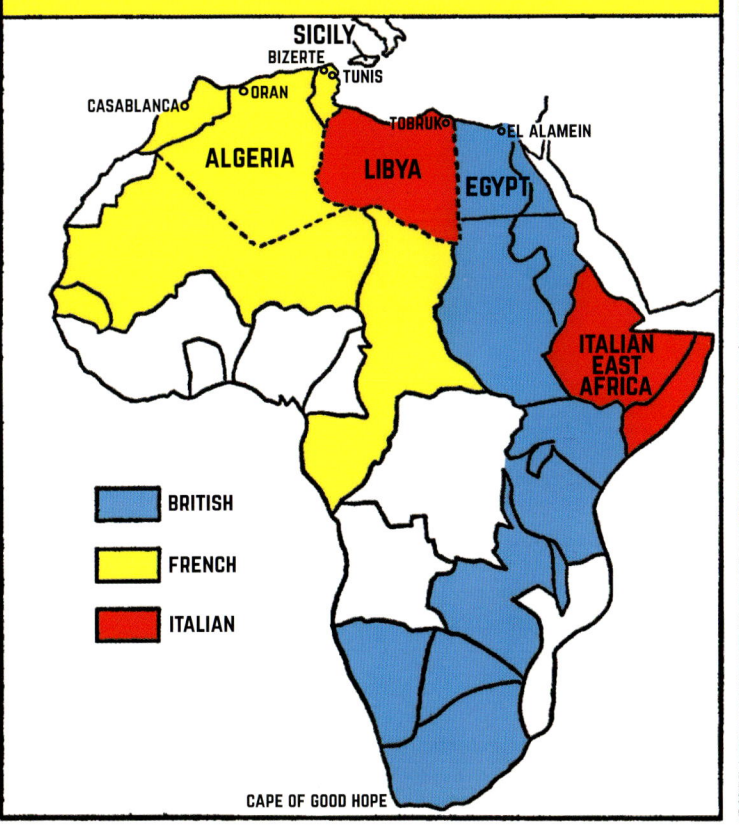

Italy invaded Egypt in September, 1940. Two months later, the British Mediterranean fleet sailed to Taranto Harbour, Italy, to attack the moored Italian Navy.

Nine British carrier planes torpedoed and sank three Italian battleships and two cruisers. In this single battle, the Italian Navy was crippled for six months.

Although outnumbered four to one, troops from Great Britain and the British Commonwealth began a drive against the invaders in December, 1940. They drove the Italians out of Egypt and deep into Libya. The Italian fortress at Tobruk fell to the British on January 22nd, 1941.

THE BRITISH ADVANCED, BUT WERE FORCED BACK UNDER A NEW ATTACK OF GERMAN TROOPS. THE GERMAN AFRIKA KORPS, UNDER THE COMMAND OF GENERAL ERWIN ROMMEL, PUSHED THE ALLIES BACK TO TOBRUK IN APRIL, 1941.
GERMAN AND ITALIAN TROOPS BESIEGED THE FORTRESS, BUT IT HELD. THE GERMANS COULD NOT GET IN, AND THE ALLIES COULD NOT GET OUT. AT LAST, IN DECEMBER, ROMMEL WITHDREW.
THE BIGGEST MILITARY PROBLEM IN NORTH AFRICA WAS SUPPLY. IN THE REGION OF BATTLE, THE LAND WAS EMPTY DESERT. SUPPLIES HAD TO COME FROM THE SEA, OR FROM BASES MANY MILES FROM THE FRONT.
NORTH AFRICA IS A TACTICIAN'S PARADISE, AND A QUARTERMASTER'S HELL.
AFTER THE FIRST WITHDRAWAL FROM TOBRUK, ROMMEL PREPARED A NEW ATTACK. THROUGH THE EARLY MONTHS OF 1942, THE HEAVILY ARMOURED GERMAN AFRIKA KORPS DROVE THE ALLIES BACK.

Then, on June 21st, 1942, the fortress at Tobruk, which had been in British hands for a year and a half, fell to Rommel's tank corps. Over 25,000 Allied soldiers were taken prisoner.

The Germans pursued the retreating Eighth Allied Army into Egypt. On July 1st, the Allies took up their position at El Alamein, only forty miles from Alexandria on the Nile River.

A change in the British high command put General Bernard Montgomery in charge of the Eighth Army.

As soon as we can break in the new tanks sent from America, we will attack Rommel. Give me a month and I will chase him out of Africa.

During July, the two armies fought to a standstill. Rommel feared his tanks would soon be outnumbered and conferred with Nazi leaders in Germany in September. Field Marshal Hermann Goering, the Air Force chief, thought little of American war production.

All the Americans can make are razor blades and refrigerators.

I only wish that we were issued similar razor blades.

| Rommel struck first, but Montgomery outguessed him. Montgomery chose the position he wished to fight from and then arranged a trick. | The trick worked. Rommel's tank corps discovered that the sand was much heavier than the map showed. Air attack and unexpectedly strong defences brought the renewed German advance to a halt. | Very short of supplies, Rommel had to retreat on September 3rd. The Eighth Army slowly built up strength. Then, under a full moon on October 23rd, 1942, almost one thousand Allied guns opened fire on the enemy. |

"SEE THAT THIS FALSE MAP FINDS ITS WAY INTO ROMMEL'S POCKET."

Under artillery and air protection, Allied infantry groups advanced to break the enemy's front. Tanks followed. For twelve days, British, Australian, Indian and New Zealand troops pounded the Afrika Korps.

At last, the Germans withdrew. Out of 240 tanks, twelve were still usable. The Germans had only enough fuel and vehicles left to transport their own men. They left thousands of Italian troops stranded in the desert to be picked up as prisoners.

As the Battle of El Alamein was being fought, 650 loaded Allied troopships were crossing the Atlantic Ocean.

"Telegraph General Montgomery. Say 'The torch is lit.'"

"Torch" was the code name for the Allied invasion of French North Africa. Just after 1am on November 8th, 1942, American and British troops hit the beaches at Casablanca, Oran and Algiers.

The Vichy government of the French colonies still supported Germany. But after three days, French resistance stopped, at the order of Admiral Henri Darlan.

In revenge, Nazi troops marched into southern France. Darlan ordered the French fleet at Toulon to be scuttled, to keep it from the Nazis. Over fifty ships were sunk.

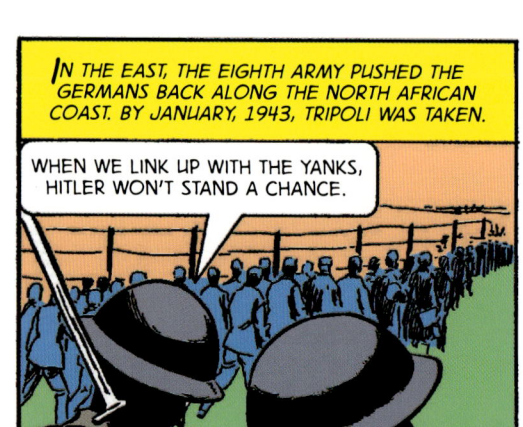

In the east, the Eighth Army pushed the Germans back along the North African coast. By January, 1943, Tripoli was taken.

"When we link up with the Yanks, Hitler won't stand a chance."

The troops of the Torch invasion drove across French North Africa to join with the Eighth Army in Tunisia. Together, they planned to sweep the Nazis into the sea.

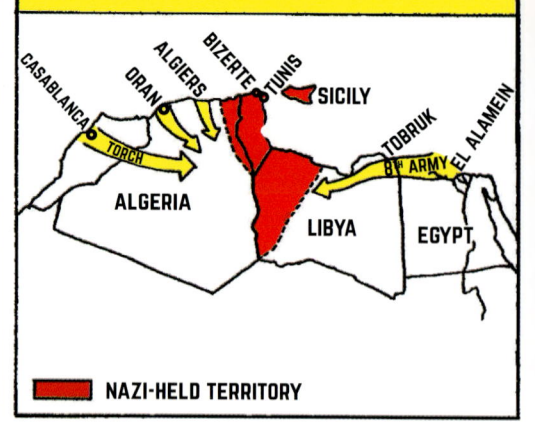

NAZI-HELD TERRITORY

In January 1943, Rommel flew to Hitler in Germany.

"North Africa is all but lost. Let us evacuate and save our men for future fighting."

"I will not retreat! Return to Africa and fight!"

The port of Tunis was particularly important to both sides because it is only seventy-five miles from Sicily. The Allies gradually pushed the Nazis into Tunis and Bizerte, but on February 14th, 1943, Rommel counterattacked.

"It is our last chance to get out of this Tunisian pocket."

The Nazis moved south and overwhelmed an American force at Kasserine Pass.

60

But Rommel had no reserves of men or materiel to replace his losses. The Nazis fought a last, desperate struggle in the northern Tunisian mountains. At Hill 609 Americans and Germans held positions sometimes only fifteen yards apart.

Then, on April 7th, an Indian patrol of the Eighth Army met a patrol from the Second Corps of the United States invasion force.

HELLO!

On May 7th, the Americans entered Bizerte and the British broke through to Tunis.

Six days later, the Axis forces surrendered. Allied aeroplanes and ships prevented any attempt to evacuate the Axis troops. More than 250,000 men were taken prisoner. Whole enemy units drove into Allied prison areas in trucks and jeeps.

YOU'D THINK THEY WERE GOING TO A PICNIC!

The Allies now controlled North Africa and had bases for an attack on Europe. Hitler was clearly on the defensive.

WAR LEADERS

HAROLD ALEXANDER

FIELD MARSHAL ALEXANDER WON RENOWN FOR HIS HANDLING OF TROOPS AT THE BRITISH WITHDRAWAL AT DUNKIRK. IN 1942, HE WAS NAMED COMMANDER-IN-CHIEF OF BRITISH FORCES IN THE MIDDLE EAST, AND SUPERVISED ALLIED FORCES IN NORTH AFRICA. LATER, HE COMMANDED THE ALLIES IN ITALY AND THE ENTIRE MEDITERRANEAN.

ERWIN ROMMEL

KNOWN AS "THE DESERT FOX" BECAUSE OF HIS CLEVER MILITARY TACTICS, FIELD MARSHAL ROMMEL WAS HITLER'S MOST SUCCESSFUL COMMANDER. AFTER LEADING AXIS FORCES IN NORTH AFRICA, HE SERVED IN ITALY AND FRANCE. IN 1944 HE COMMITTED SUICIDE AFTER BEING CAUGHT IN AN ARMY PLOT AGAINST HITLER.

MARK W. CLARK

LATE IN 1942, GENERAL CLARK LED A SECRET AMERICAN MILITARY MISSION INTO ALGERIA TO PREPARE THE WAY FOR THE ALLIED LANDINGS. LATER, AS COMMANDER OF THE AMERICAN-BRITISH FIFTH ARMY, HE LED THE INVASIONS OF SICILY AND ITALY.

THE ITALIAN CAMPAIGN

With the Axis driven from Africa, the Allies were set to strike at the mainland of Europe. But first they had to capture a vital stepping stone to the continent - the island of Sicily.

On July 9th, 1943, a great Allied armada of nearly three thousand ships massed in the Mediterranean.

The Nazis on Sicily expected an attack on the western end of the island, but the Allies hit the beaches on the east and south.

Six American divisions, seven British divisions and a Canadian force quickly gained a strong foothold. The Nazis retreated north, blasting bridges and mountain roads behind them.

In mid-August, the Nazis gave up Sicily and evacuated sixty thousand troops to Italy.

IN ITALY, THERE WAS GREAT UNREST. ALLIED PLANES WERE BOMBING THE CITIES, THE PEOPLE HAD LITTLE FOOD, AND THE ECONOMY WAS SHATTERED.

"MUSSOLINI PROMISED US AN EMPIRE, BUT NOW HE CAN'T GIVE US BREAD!"

IN JULY 1943, MUSSOLINI MET WITH HITLER, WHO URGED HIM TO KEEP A STRONG HOLD ON ITALY.

"BUT I HAVE JUST HEARD THAT ROME IS BEING BOMBED. WE ARE BEING BEATEN, FUEHRER."

ON JULY 24TH, ITALY'S GOVERNING BODY, THE FASCIST GRAND COUNCIL, VOTED TO OUST MUSSOLINI IN FAVOUR OF KING VICTOR EMMANUEL III. MUSSOLINI WENT TO THE KING AND ASKED HIS SUPPORT.

"MY DEAR DUCE, IT IS NO LONGER ANY USE. ITALY HAS GONE TO BITS. THE SOLDIERS DON'T WANT TO FIGHT ANY MORE. AT THIS MOMENT, YOU ARE THE MOST HATED MAN IN ITALY."

MUSSOLINI WAS ARRESTED, BUT LATER ESCAPED TO NORTHERN ITALY. MARSHAL PIETRO BADOGLIO WAS NAMED HEAD OF THE ITALIAN GOVERNMENT. IN SEPTEMBER, HE BROADCAST A MESSAGE TO HIS PEOPLE.

"ITALY HAS SURRENDERED UNCONDITIONALLY TO THE ALLIES. WE MUST NOW JOIN THEM TO FIGHT THE GERMANS IN EVERY WAY."

Although the Italians had surrendered, Italy was still held by German forces. After softening up Nazi airfields and military centres through air attacks, the Allies invaded Italy in early September.

On September 3rd, two British divisions ploughed ashore at Reggio di Calabria. By the end of the month, they controlled the Italian southern peninsula.

ITALY
ROME ⊙ ○ CASSINO
ANZIO
INVASION BY FIFTH ARMY, SEPT. 9TH → ○ SALERNO
INVASION BY BRITISH EIGHTH ARMY, SEPT. 3RD → ○ REGGIO DI CALABRIA
SICILY

On September 9th, a large British-American force, the Fifth Army, hit the beaches north of Salerno.

THE GERMANS BOMBARDED THE SALERNO INVADERS WITH AN ARTILLERY BARRAGE FROM HILLS OVERLOOKING THE BEACHHEAD. MANY ALLIED SOLDIERS FELL ONLY A FEW MOMENTS AFTER REACHING SHORE.

THE ALLIED TROOPS DUG IN. AMERICAN GENERAL MARK CLARK, THE FIFTH ARMY COMMANDER, CALLED FOR MORE AIR SUPPORT.

THE SHELLING IS EXTREMELY HEAVY. SEND OVER MORE PLANES.

A LARGE FORCE OF PLANES FROM BASES IN SICILY AND NORTH AFRICA CAME IN TO BOMB AND MACHINE GUN THE NAZI ARTILLERY.

THE COMBINED AIR AND GROUND ATTACKS FORCED THE NAZIS BACK. BY OCTOBER, THE ALLIES CONTROLLED THE SOUTHERN THIRD OF ITALY AND HAD ENTERED NAPLES.

THE NAZIS FELL BACK TO A LINE ABOUT ONE HUNDRED MILES SOUTH OF ROME. IN LATE JANUARY, CLARK DECIDED TO MAKE A SURPRISE MOVE.

WE'LL BYPASS THE BATTLE LINE AND CONVOY TWO DIVISIONS TO ANZIO BY SEA. IT'S ONLY THIRTY MILES FROM ROME.

SEVENTY THOUSAND ALLIED TROOPS LANDED AT ANZIO BEACH. THE INVADERS RECEIVED A HEAVY NAZI ARTILLERY BARRAGE FROM THE SURROUNDING HILLS. THERE WERE MANY ALLIED CASUALTIES.

THE ALLIES WERE PINNED DOWN AT ANZIO FOR FOUR MONTHS. THEN THEY BROKE OUT. THEY MOVED SOUTHEAST TO ATTACK CASSINO, BUT MADE LITTLE PROGRESS. THE NAZIS, ATOP MONTE CASSINO, HAD A COMMANDING ADVANTAGE OVER THE ALLIED TROOPS BELOW.

FROM HERE, WE CAN HOLD OUT FOR MONTHS. NO ONE CAN COME UP THOSE ROADS AGAINST OUR FIRE.

THE ALLIES WISHED TO AVOID BOMBING MONTE CASSINO BECAUSE OF ITS ANCIENT AND SACRED MONASTERY. FINALLY, A DECISION WAS MADE.

INFORM AIR COMMAND TO BOMB THE MONASTERY.

ALLIED PLANES REDUCED THE MONASTERY TO RUBBLE AND DESTROYED MANY NAZI FORTIFICATIONS. FINALLY, IN MID-MAY, 1944, A POLISH* BRIGADE PLANTED ITS FLAG ATOP MONTE CASSINO.	THEIR STRONGEST DEFENSIVE POSITION TAKEN, THE NAZIS RETREATED. THE ALLIED ARMIES MOVED NORTH. ON JUNE 4TH, CLARK AND HIS TROOPS ENTERED ROME TO A WILD WELCOME FROM THE ITALIAN PEOPLE.

*AFTER THE FALL OF POLAND, A FREE POLISH GROUP WAS ORGANISED IN ENGLAND.

IN AUGUST, THE BRITISH ENTERED FLORENCE, ON THE ARNO RIVER. THEY FOUND THAT THE RETREATING NAZIS HAD DESTROYED MANY OF THE CITY'S BEAUTIFUL BUILDINGS AND BRIDGES.

"THERE'S JUST ONE BRIDGE LEFT STANDING. THE GERMANS HAVE RANSACKED THE HOSPITALS, TOO. IT'S BEEN THE SAME ALL THROUGH ITALY."

HITLER WAS DETERMINED TO HOLD THE ALLIES IN ITALY FOR AS LONG AS POSSIBLE. IT WAS NOT UNTIL APRIL 29TH, 1945, NEARLY A YEAR AFTER THE CAPTURE OF MONTE CASSINO, THAT THE NAZI FORCES IN ITALY SURRENDERED.

BLOCKBUSTERS AND BUZZ BOMBS

ON MAY 20TH, 1942, MORE THAN ONE THOUSAND BRITISH PLANES ATTACKED THE GERMAN CITY OF COLOGNE WITH BLOCKBUSTERS, HUGE BOMBS WEIGHING AS MUCH AS SIX TONS APIECE. FROM THEN ON, MASS ALLIED RAIDS WERE COMMON. IN JULY 1943, EIGHT THOUSAND TONS OF BOMBS FELL ON HAMBURG, DESTROYING THREE-QUARTERS OF THE CITY. BY EARLY 1944, THE BOMBINGS GREATLY AFFECTED NAZI WAR PRODUCTION AND REDUCED THE AMOUNT OF ARMS AVAILABLE TO HITLER'S TROOPS.

IN MID-1944, THE NAZIS UNLEASHED A NEW WEAPON, THE V-1, SHORT FOR VERGELTUNGSWAFFE EINS, OR "REVENGE WEAPON ONE." THE ENGLISH CALLED IT THE "BUZZ BOMB." IT WAS A SMALL, PILOTLESS, JET-PROPELLED PLANE CARRYING A TON OF EXPLOSIVES. FROM FRANCE, THE NAZIS DIRECTED THEIR V-1s AT ENGLAND, CAUSING MANY DEATHS AND DESTROYING MANY BUILDINGS.

*THE DOODLEBUG

THE NORMANDY INVASION

The Allies had hoped that success in Italy would liberate troops for fighting on other fronts. A massive invasion of Nazi-held territory in Western Europe was planned for the spring of 1944. In preparation, two hundred thousand Allied troops were transported to England.

In late May, General Eisenhower, the invasion's Supreme Commander, made a final inspection of the Allied invasion troops.

"We'll soon know if their fighting is as good as their training."

Eisenhower selected June 6th as D-Day, the day of invasion. In the early morning hours, British bombers began attacking Nazi defences on the Normandy coast of France.

At the same time, Allied paratroopers landed to the north and south of the beaches where the main invasion force was to come ashore.

The paratroopers formed a line around the beaches to keep the Nazis away from the main force.

AT DAWN, FIVE THOUSAND ALLIED SHIPS STEAMED TOWARDS THE NORMANDY SHORE.	THE LARGER WARSHIPS SHELLED NAZI COASTAL DEFENCES.
OVERHEAD, AIR COVER OF NINE THOUSAND PLANES BOMBED AND STRAFED NAZI POSITIONS JUST BEYOND THE LANDING AREA.	H-HOUR, THE HOUR OF LANDING, WAS 6:30AM. THE FIRST TROOPS LEFT THEIR LANDING BARGES AND WADED ASHORE.

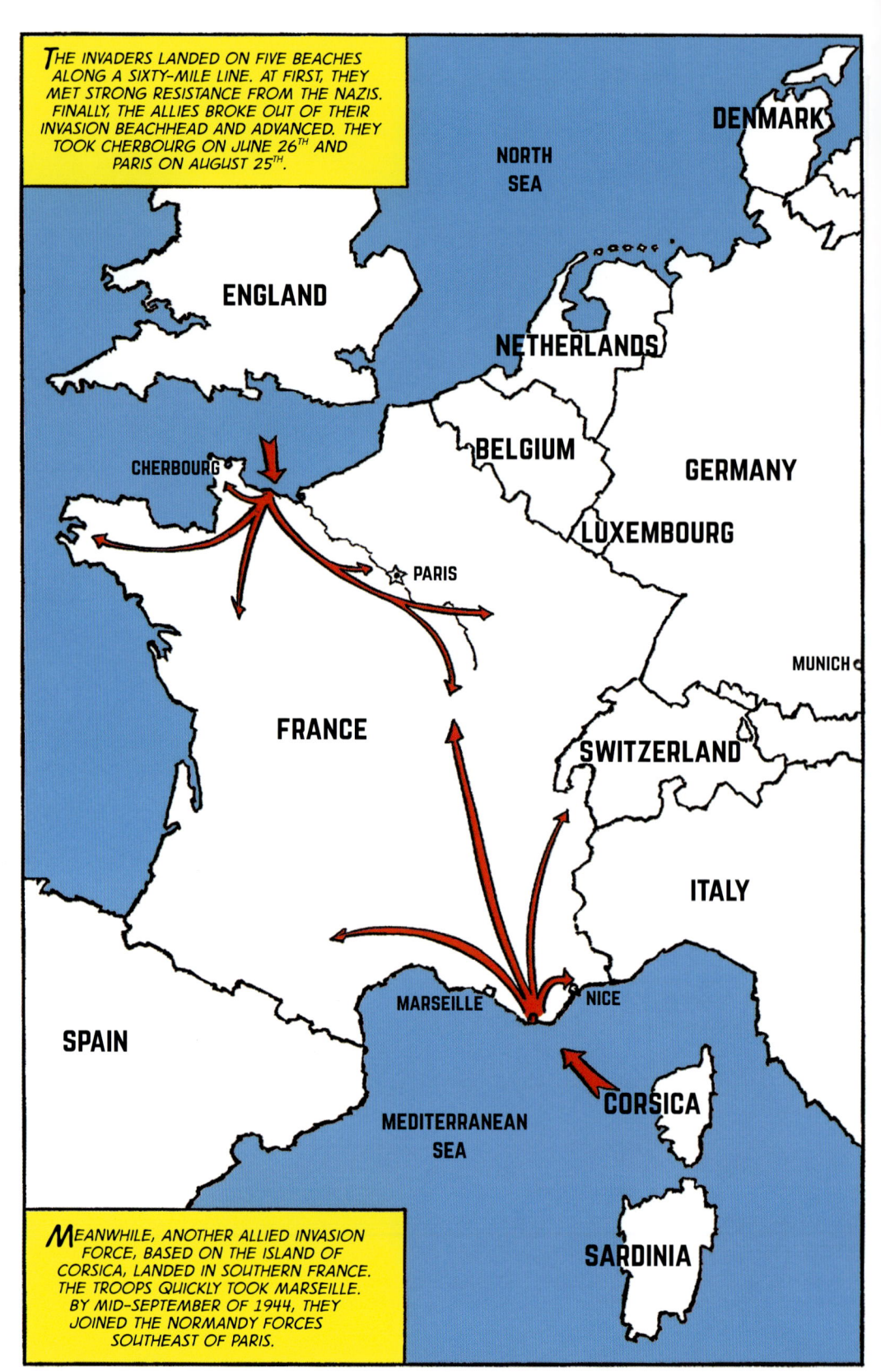

The invaders landed on five beaches along a sixty-mile line. At first, they met strong resistance from the Nazis. Finally, the Allies broke out of their invasion beachhead and advanced. They took Cherbourg on June 26th and Paris on August 25th.

Meanwhile, another Allied invasion force, based on the island of Corsica, landed in southern France. The troops quickly took Marseille. By mid-September of 1944, they joined the Normandy forces southeast of Paris.

THE BATTLE OF THE BULGE

PART OF THE NORMANDY INVASION FORCE SWEPT INTO BELGIUM. BY DECEMBER 16TH, 1944, ALLIED TROOPS IN BELGIUM THREATENED THE GERMAN BORDER. THE NAZIS MASSED TWENTY-FIVE DIVISIONS FOR A THRUST INTO THE ARDENNES, A SECTION IN SOUTHERN BELGIUM AND NORTHERN LUXEMBOURG. IN COMMAND WAS FIELD MARSHAL GERD VON RUNDSTEDT.

We will advance on a forty-five mile front. Our heaviest force will go through Bastogne, Belgium.

THE NAZI DRIVE CAUGHT THE OPPOSING AMERICAN ARMIES BY SURPRISE. THEY WERE FORCED BACK.

VON RUNDSTEDT'S TROOPS CARVED OUT A BULGE OF TERRITORY SIXTY-FIVE MILES WIDE. HOWEVER, IN THE CENTRE OF THE BULGE, AT BASTOGNE, HIS TANKS WERE STOPPED BY AMERICAN ARMOURED FORCES.

If we cannot take Bastogne by direct assault, then we will encircle it.

CRACK NAZI LEGIONS MOVED TO THE NORTH AND SOUTH OF BASTOGNE AND SHATTERED THE CITY WITH ARTILLERY FIRE. GENERAL EISENHOWER SENT IN THE 101ST AIRBORNE DIVISION. THEIR PLANES GROUNDED BECAUSE OF BAD WEATHER, THE MEN SPED INTO BASTOGNE IN TRUCKS, JUST BEATING THE APPROACHING GERMANS.

FIGHTING WAS BITTER FOR THE NEXT FEW DAYS. THEN TWO GERMANS, UNDER A FLAG OF TRUCE, CAME INTO BASTOGNE TO DEMAND THAT THE AMERICANS SURRENDER. AN AMERICAN COLONEL TOOK THE DEMAND TO GENERAL ANTHONY McAULIFFE, ALLIED COMMANDER AT BASTOGNE.
WHAT SHALL I TELL THEM?
NUTS!

THE REPLY WAS HANDED TO THE GERMANS. THEY WERE CONFUSED BY McAULIFFE'S MESSAGE.
I DO NOT UNDERSTAND THIS WORD "NUTS".
IN PLAIN ENGLISH, IT IS THE SAME AS "GO TO HELL".

MEANWHILE, A STRONG AMERICAN ARMOURED FORCE, LED BY LIEUTENANT-GENERAL GEORGE PATTON, MOVED TOWARDS THE BULGE FROM THE SOUTH.
LET'S GO. WE'VE GOT TO RELIEVE McAULIFFE.

ALLIED PLANES HAD BEEN GROUNDED FOR A WEEK BECAUSE OF BAD WEATHER. BUT ON DECEMBER 23RD, THE SKIES CLEARED. FIVE THOUSAND ALLIED BOMBERS FLEW OVER THE NAZI LINES AND DESTROYED MANY FUEL AND AMMUNITION DUMPS.

THE AMERICANS AT BASTOGNE WERE GREATLY OUTNUMBERED, BUT THEY HELD ON. THE NAZIS LAUNCHED SEVERAL ATTACKS ON CHRISTMAS DAY.

THIS MAKES THE FOURTH ATTACK SINCE LUNCH. SOME MERRY CHRISTMAS!

THE NEXT DAY, PATTON'S TANKS ARRIVED. THEY BROKE THROUGH AND RELIEVED THE DEFENDERS, BUT THE NAZIS STILL HELD MOST OF THE BULGE. ON NEW YEAR'S DAY, 1945, NAZI PLANES STRUCK ALL ALLIED AIRFIELDS NEAR THE BATTLE FRONT.

MANY ALLIED PLANES WERE DESTROYED, BUT WERE QUICKLY REPLACED. HOWEVER, THE NAZIS HAD NO MORE PLANES TO REPLACE THE ONES LOST IN THE RAIDS. VON RUNDSTEDT KNEW HIS CAUSE WAS DESPERATE.

WE ARE BEING CLOSED IN. ORDER A WITHDRAWAL TO THE EAST OF BASTOGNE.

FROM THE NORTH, AMERICAN AND BRITISH TROOPS, LED BY FIELD MARSHAL MONTGOMERY, ADVANCED TO JOIN WITH PATTON'S TANKMEN. BY MID-JANUARY, THE NAZIS WERE DRIVEN OUT OF THE BULGE, AND THE ALLIES WERE SET TO DELIVER THE KNOCKOUT BLOW TO HITLER'S GERMANY.

VICTORY IN EUROPE

Early in 1945, time and manpower ran out for Hitler. In the West, the Allies had liberated France and crossed into Germany. Allied troops were slowly pushing north in Italy. To the east, the Russians had thrown the Nazis back from Stalingrad and were now on German soil.

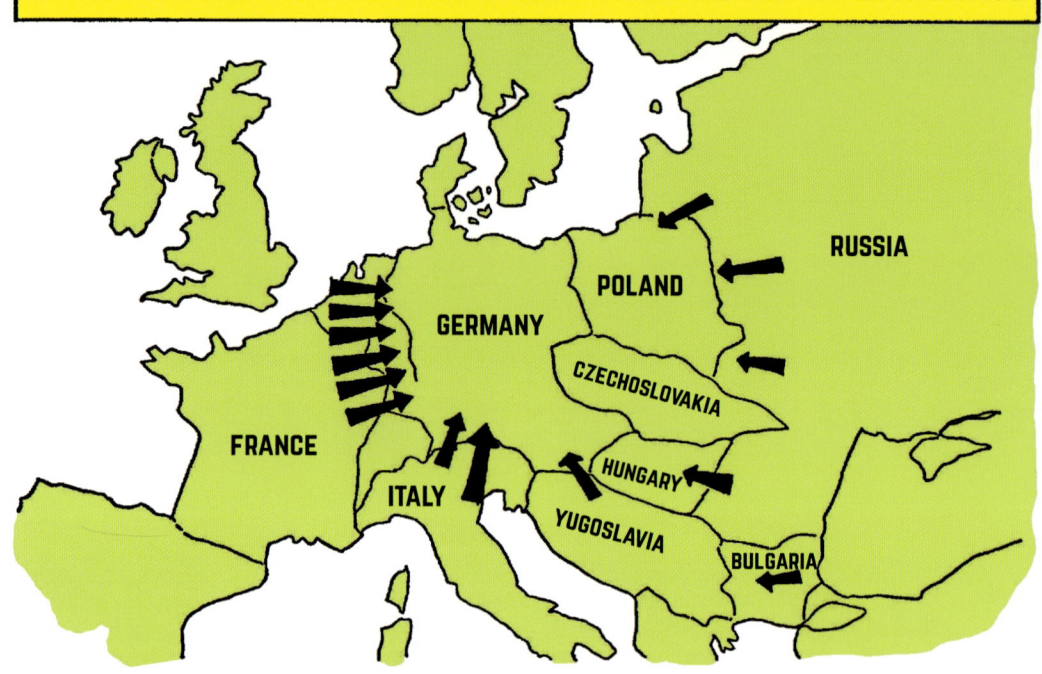

The Allied forces in Europe now numbered ten million men. On January 1st, 1945, Hitler broadcast to the German people.

"The end of the war will not come before 1946 unless by a German victory, because Germany will never capitulate."

In late February, the entire Western Allied line swept to the banks of the Rhine River. The retreating Nazis blew up dozens of bridges across the river. General Eisenhower foresaw trouble in crossing it.

"If we can seize just one bridge intact, it will save both lives and time."

ON MARCH 7TH, AN AMERICAN PLATOON APPROACHED THE BRIDGE AT REMAGEN, ON THE RHINE.

THE BRIDGE IS STILL THERE! THEY HAVEN'T BLOWN IT UP YET!

THE PLATOON RACED ACROSS THE BRIDGE THROUGH HEAVY NAZI FIRE FROM THE OTHER SIDE. MIDWAY ACROSS, THE AMERICANS WERE STUNNED BY AN EXPLOSION.

DYNAMITE! SHE'LL COLLAPSE ANY MINUTE!

BUT THE BRIDGE STAYED INTACT. ONLY ONE OF THE CHARGES PLANTED BY THE NAZIS HAD EXPLODED. THE MAIN CHARGE HAD FAILED TO GO OFF. IN TWENTY-FOUR HOURS, MORE THAN EIGHT THOUSAND AMERICAN SOLDIERS CROSSED THE RHINE.

THE BRIDGE RUINED DEFENCE PLANS FOR GERMANY. NAZI TROOPS WERE CALLED AWAY FROM OTHER RHINE POSITIONS TO FIGHT THE AMERICANS CROSSING AT REMAGEN.

WE CANNOT DEFEND EVERY KEY POINT ON THE RIVER. WE SIMPLY LACK THE MEN.

WITH TROOPS ON BOTH SIDES OF THE RHINE, AMERICAN ARMY ENGINEERS WENT TO WORK. IN A FEW DAYS, THEY BUILT SIXTY-TWO FLOATING BRIDGES. BY MARCH 25TH, SEVEN ALLIED ARMIES HAD CROSSED THE RIVER.

TWO AMERICAN ARMIES RACED INTO THE RUHR AND IN A WEEK, CAPTURED FOUR HUNDRED THOUSAND NAZIS. GENERAL PATTON'S TANKS SPED OVER SOUTHERN GERMAN HIGHWAYS AND REACHED CZECHOSLOVAKIA ON APRIL 23RD.

MEANWHILE, RUSSIAN ARMIES NEARED WARSAW. IN THE CITY, THE POLISH RESISTANCE, OBEYING ORDERS FROM MOSCOW, CAME INTO THE OPEN TO FIGHT THE NAZIS. THE PATRIOTS QUICKLY CAPTURED SEVERAL DISTRICTS.

WHILE THE RUSSIANS ARE ATTACKING, WE CAN DO THE GERMANS A LOT OF DAMAGE.

SUDDENLY, THE RUSSIANS HALTED OUTSIDE WARSAW. THE NAZIS HAD TIME TO CONCENTRATE THEIR FIRE ON THE POLES. THEY KILLED 250,000 CIVILIANS.

WARSAW FELL TO THE RUSSIANS ON JANUARY 17TH, 1945; BUDAPEST ON FEBRUARY 13TH; AND VIENNA ON APRIL 13TH. EIGHT DAYS LATER, SOVIET TROOPS REACHED THE OUTSKIRTS OF BERLIN.

ON APRIL 25TH, AMERICAN TROOPS SEVENTY MILES SOUTH OF BERLIN SIGHTED AN ADVANCING ARMY.

WHO'S THAT HEADING TOWARDS US? GERMANS?

NO! RUSSIANS!

THE TWO FORCES SALUTED EACH OTHER. A RUSSIAN MAJOR MADE A SPEECH.

TODAY IS THE HAPPIEST DAY OF OUR LIVES. NOW AT LAST WE MEET ONE ANOTHER, AND THIS IS THE END OF OUR ENEMY.

IN ITALY, THE ALLIED FIFTH ARMY OVERCAME THE FINAL NAZI RESISTANCE. ON APRIL 29TH, THE GERMAN ARMIES IN ITALY SURRENDERED AT THE HEADQUARTERS OF BRITISH FIELD MARSHAL HAROLD ALEXANDER, ALLIED COMMANDER IN ITALY.

HOW MANY GERMANS ARE SURRENDERING?

OUR REMAINING FORCES IN ITALY NUMBER ALMOST ONE MILLION. ALL WILL LAY DOWN THEIR ARMS.

ITALIAN PARTISANS FOUND THE ESCAPED MUSSOLINI IN A FARMHOUSE. HE WAS SHOT TO DEATH, THEN HANGED BY HIS HEELS, WITH OTHER FASCISTS, OUTSIDE A MILAN FILLING STATION.

IN HIS UNDERGROUND HIDEOUT IN BERLIN, HITLER FELT HIS EMPIRE CRUMBLE. MANY OF HIS FOLLOWERS DESERTED HIM. ON APRIL 30TH, IT IS BELIEVED THAT HE SHOT HIMSELF AND HAD HIS BODY BURNED. THE NAZI COMMAND WAS TAKEN OVER BY ADMIRAL KARL DOENITZ.

THE *FUEHRER* IS DEAD.

ON MAY 2ND, DOENITZ OFFERED TO SURRENDER IN THE WEST IF HE WERE ALLOWED TO CONTINUE FIGHTING THE RUSSIANS IN THE EAST. FIELD MARSHAL MONTGOMERY, SPEAKING FOR THE ALLIES, REFUSED.

INFORM THE ADMIRAL THAT WE DEMAND UNCONDITIONAL SURRENDER ON ALL FRONTS.

THE NAZIS SURRENDERED UNCONDITIONALLY ON MAY 7TH AT EISENHOWER'S HEADQUARTERS IN REIMS, FRANCE. AT 12:01AM, MAY 9TH, 1945 ALL SHOOTING STOPPED. THE WAR IN EUROPE WAS OVER.

WAR LEADERS

DWIGHT D. EISENHOWER

AFTER COMMANDING THE ALLIED INVASION OF NORTH AFRICA, GENERAL EISENHOWER DIRECTED THE INVASIONS OF SICILY AND ITALY. IN 1944, HE WAS NAMED SUPREME COMMANDER OF THE ALLIED FORCES INVADING FRANCE.

BERNARD MONTGOMERY

FIELD MARSHAL MONTGOMERY BECAME THE HERO OF NORTH AFRICA WHEN HIS BRITISH EIGHTH ARMY DEFEATED THE NAZI AFRIKA KORPS AT EL ALAMEIN. FOR D-DAY, HE WAS PUT IN COMMAND OF ALL BRITISH FORCES IN WESTERN EUROPE.

OMAR BRADLEY

GENERAL BRADLEY COMMANDED THE SECOND ARMY CORPS IN TUNISIA AND SICILY. IN 1944, HE LED THE AMERICAN ADVANCE OUT OF NORMANDY. HE WAS RESPONSIBLE FOR ALL AMERICAN GROUND FORCES IN FRANCE, COMMANDING ABOUT ONE MILLION MEN.

LEYTE GULF

The war in the Pacific took a more roundabout course. The Allies followed a policy of "island hopping". Key islands held by the Japanese were chosen as targets. When these were won they were used as supply bases for attacking the next targets.

From the Hawaiian Islands and from New Guinea, the Allies cut into the Japanese front. When Guam was liberated on August 10th, 1944, the Allies had bases from which super bombers could reach Japan.

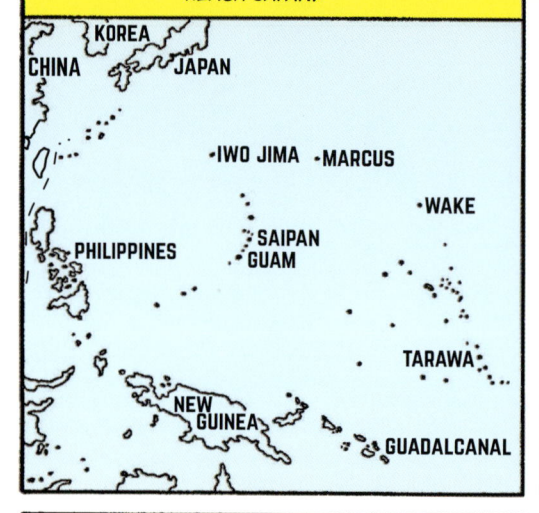

The next major objective was the Philippine Islands, held by Japan. On October 20th, 1944, four divisions of American troops landed on Leyte, a central island, protected by guns and planes of the Seventh United States Fleet.

The commander of the Japanese fleet planned to destroy the United States ships covering the landing. Then the small American force could be wiped out by Japanese ground troops.

We will attack in three parts. The Northern Force will sail from Japan and decoy the Third United States Fleet, which has the heaviest battleships, north of the landing on Leyte.

Our Centre Force will approach Leyte Gulf from the north, through San Bernardino Strait. Our Southern Force will come up to Leyte from the south, through Surigao Strait. There, our two fleets will crush the remainder of the American fleet between them, and we will keep the Philippines.

82

ON OCTOBER 23RD, AMERICAN SUBMARINES DISCOVERED THE JAPANESE CENTRE FORCE WEST OF THE PHILIPPINES. THEY SANK TWO CRUISERS AND DAMAGED ANOTHER.

THE NEXT DAY, NORTHWEST OF LEYTE GULF, AMERICAN PLANES SANK A GIANT JAPANESE BATTLESHIP. THE JAPANESE CENTRE FORCE TURNED BACK. ADMIRAL WILLIAM HALSEY, COMMANDER OF THE THIRD UNITED STATES FLEET, WAS SURE OF THE VICTORY.

GOOD. THE SEVENTH FLEET CAN HANDLE THOSE JAPANESE SHIPS YOU SIGHTED AT SURIGAO. BUT WHERE DO ALL THE JAPANESE PLANES THAT ATTACKED US TODAY COME FROM?

LATE THAT AFTERNOON, SEARCH PLANES SPOTTED THE DECOY JAPANESE FLEET SAILING FROM THE NORTH.

FOUR CARRIERS, TWO BATTLESHIPS, THREE CRUISERS AND TEN DESTROYERS! IF WE COULD PUT THEM OUT OF ACTION, THE JAPANESE NAVY WOULD BE FINISHED.

SINCE THE CENTRAL FORCE HAD TURNED BACK, HALSEY THOUGHT THAT THE NORTHERN PASSAGE TO LEYTE WAS SAFE FROM ATTACK. HE FOLLOWED THE NORTHERN JAPANESE FORCE TO THE NORTH, LEAVING SAN BERNARDINO STRAIT UNGUARDED.

But as Halsey's fleet sailed away, the Japanese Centre Force turned around once again, and headed right back towards the strait, unopposed.

At the same time, the Southern Japanese Force was approaching Leyte Gulf from the south. That night, a task force of the Seventh United States Fleet, under Rear Admiral Jesse Oldendorf, engaged the Southern Force in a fierce battle.

The first part of the Japanese fleet was completely shattered. Oldendorf's force sank two battleships and two destroyers. The rest of the Japanese ships tried to slip through to Leyte in the darkness, but at last they turned back.

Although the Southern Force was destroyed, the Centre Force took an easy passage through San Bernardino Strait. Then...

A STRONG ENEMY FLEET SIGHTED DEAD AHEAD!

84

THE JAPANESE WERE MISTAKEN. THE AMERICAN SHIPS WERE ONLY LIGHTLY ARMED CARRIERS AND DESTROYERS, ESCORTS OF THE AMERICAN LANDING FORCES ON LEYTE.

ORDER ALL SHIPS TO BREAK FORMATION AND ATTACK SEPARATELY.

THE JAPANESE HAD NO ORGANISED PLAN. AMERICAN DESTROYERS MOVED IN. ONE, THE JOHNSTON, DODGED HEAVY FIRE AND TORPEDOED A CRUISER, PUTTING HER OUT OF THE FIGHT.

ALONE, THE JOHNSTON THEN ATTACKED FOUR JAPANESE DESTROYERS AND A CRUISER.

OTHER LONE AMERICAN DESTROYERS TOOK ON JAPANESE BATTLESHIPS. THIS GAVE MOST OF THE AMERICAN ESCORT CARRIERS TIME TO ESCAPE, ALTHOUGH TWO WERE SUNK.

WHILE FLEEING, SOME OF THE CARRIERS MANAGED TO LAUNCH PLANES. THEY SANK TWO JAPANESE CRUISERS. THE CENTRE FORCE TURNED BACK.

WE MUST RETREAT BEFORE THE AMERICANS SEND IN REINFORCEMENTS.

DURING THIS TIME, THE THIRD UNITED STATES FLEET WAS STILL PURSUING THE DECOY JAPANESE FORCE IN THE NORTH.

"WE WILL PROBABLY BE WIPED OUT, BUT WE HAVE LURED THE MAIN FORCE OF THE ENEMY NAVY FAR AWAY FROM LEYTE GULF."

THEN, HALSEY BEGAN RECEIVING RADIO MESSAGES FROM THE EXHAUSTED SEVENTH FLEET.

"URGENT, SIR. ADMIRAL KINKAID IS UNDER HEAVY ENEMY ATTACK AND REQUESTS IMMEDIATE AID."

HALSEY TURNED BACK TO SAN BERNARDINO STRAIT WITH HIS FASTEST BATTLESHIPS, LEAVING TWO CARRIER GROUPS TO CHASE THE NORTHERN FORCE. AT DAWN ON OCTOBER 25TH, PLANES TOOK OFF FROM THE REMAINING AMERICAN CARRIERS.

"FOUR JAPANESE CARRIERS AND ABOUT A DOZEN OTHER SHIPS. WE SHOULD BE GETTING SOME HITS TODAY."

AT 8:30AM, THE FIRST AMERICAN TORPEDO AND DIVE BOMBERS ATTACKED. A JAPANESE CARRIER RECEIVED SEVERAL DIRECT BOMB HITS AND SANK IN LESS THAN AN HOUR.

ONE GROUP OF FORTY AMERICAN PLANES CONCENTRATED ON THE LARGEST JAPANESE CARRIER. THREE TORPEDOES BLASTED HER ALMOST AT THE SAME TIME. SHE SANK IN THE EARLY AFTERNOON.

HALSEY, WHO HAD RACED BACK TO SAN BERNARDINO STRAIT, FOUND THAT HE WAS TOO LATE. THE JAPANESE CENTRE FORCE, ALL THAT WAS NOW LEFT OF THE FLEET ATTACKING LEYTE GULF, HAD SLIPPED THROUGH IN SAFETY.

NEVER MIND. WE'LL GET AFTER THEM TOMORROW IN PLANES.

THE NEXT DAY, AMERICAN CARRIER PLANES SANK A CRUISER AND TWO DESTROYERS OF THE RETREATING CENTRAL FORCE. AT LAST, THE BATTLE FOR LEYTE GULF WAS OVER. THE ALLIED LAND INVASION OF THE PHILIPPINES COULD BEGIN IN EARNEST.

DURING THE BATTLE, JAPAN HAD LOST TWENTY-SIX SHIPS. THE AMERICAN LOSS WAS SIX SHIPS. LEYTE COST JAPAN ALMOST ALL OF HER REMAINING SEA POWER.

THE MAINLAND WAR

It took the Allies six months, until the end of February, 1945, to free the Philippines. The islands were important as bases from which to attack Japanese fortifications in China.

The Japanese had closed off the major land supply route to China when they captured the Burma Road in 1942. In 1943, British, Chinese and American troops began hacking their way through thick jungles to build another supply road.
It was completed in January, 1945.

All the time that the Burma Road was closed, supplies reached China by air from India, over "The Hump", a dangerous route over the Himalayan mountains.

The United States built air bases on unoccupied Chinese territory to fight the Japanese. All through the war, the American Volunteer Group, the "Flying Tigers", flew bombing missions against the Japanese.

WAR LEADERS

LOUIS MOUNTBATTEN

EARLY IN THE WAR, ADMIRAL MOUNTBATTEN PLANNED BRITISH COMMANDO RAIDS AGAINST THE NAZIS IN FRANCE. IN 1943, HE BECAME SUPREME ALLIED COMMANDER IN SOUTHEAST ASIA, WHERE HE LED THE FIGHT TO RETAKE BURMA AND MALAYA.

HIDEKI TOJO

AS THE JAPANESE WAR PREMIER, TOJO GUIDED HIS COUNTRY IN ITS PLANS OF CONQUEST. IN 1944, AFTER NUMEROUS ALLIED VICTORIES IN THE PACIFIC, HE WAS FORCED TO RESIGN.

CHESTER NIMITZ

ADMIRAL NIMITZ TOOK COMMAND OF THE AMERICAN PACIFIC FLEET SHORTLY AFTER THE ATTACK ON PEARL HARBOUR. HE DIRECTED ALL NAVY AND MARINE OPERATIONS AND PLANNED THE INVASIONS OF JAPAN'S PACIFIC STRONGHOLDS.

IWO JIMA AND OKINAWA

Needing airfields closer to Japan, the Americans prepared to invade Iwo Jima, an island only 750 miles from Tokyo. For seventy-four days, the island was pounded by American planes and ships. On February 19th, 1945, thirty thousand Marines landed. The fighting was bloody. On March 15th, the American flag was raised on Mount Suribachi, the final Japanese stronghold. Four thousand Marines and twenty-one thousand Japanese died in the struggle.

The airfield on Okinawa Island was the base from which suicide missions of Japanese planes attacked the Allies. On April 1st, one hundred thousand American soldiers and Marines hit the beaches at Okinawa, only 362 miles from the Japanese home islands. Okinawa is rocky, and the Japanese defenders hid in caves and pillboxes, steel and concrete bunkers for machine gunners. Most of the men preferred death to surrender. It took the Allies over three months of hard fighting to put down the enemy resistance.

VICTORY IN THE PACIFIC

Many pilots of the Japanese air force volunteered to crash their explosive-filled planes into American ships. Such pilots were called kamikazes. Before they took off, they drank a final toast to the Japanese emperor.

"I DRINK TO THE EMPEROR AND TO A GLORIOUS DEATH."

The largest kamikaze attack took place off Okinawa. Hundreds of kamikazes attacked 1,500 Allied ships. On May 14th, twenty-four kamikazes headed for the carrier "Enterprise". Twenty-three were shot down or missed their target.

The last kamikaze, carrying a six hundred-pound bomb, smashed into the centre of the carrier.

Fire fighters saved the Enterprise. Kamikazes sank thirty-four American ships and damaged 288 others during the war's last months.

"LOOK AT THEM COME. THEY'D RATHER DIE THAN SURRENDER!"

MEANWHILE, AMERICAN B-29 BOMBERS STRUCK AT JAPANESE CITIES. TOKYO WAS BOMBED EVERY DAY.

IN JULY, GENERAL DOUGLAS MACARTHUR MADE PLANS TO INVADE THE JAPANESE HOME ISLANDS.

We will use Okinawa as our main base. Plan on early November.

THEN, ON JULY 16TH, A TREMENDOUS BLAST SHOOK THE NEW MEXICO DESERT IN THE UNITED STATES. THE FIRST ATOMIC BOMB HAD BEEN EXPLODED.

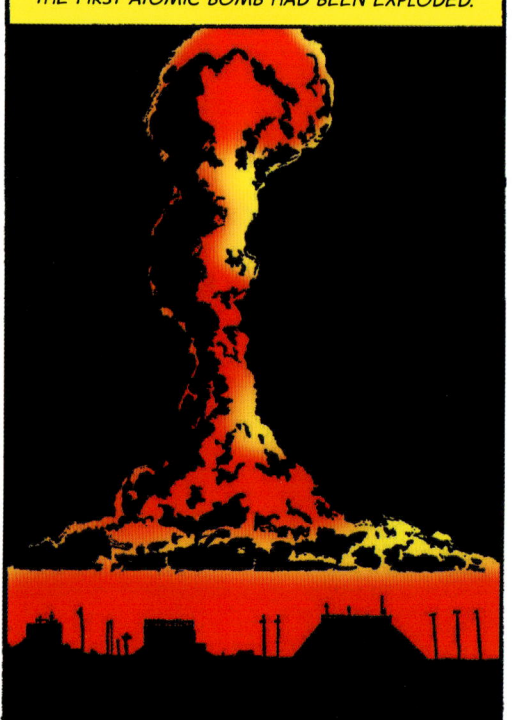

IN WASHINGTON, D.C., AMERICAN SECRETARY OF WAR, HENRY L. STIMSON, URGED PRESIDENT TRUMAN TO USE THE BOMB AGAINST JAPAN.

Invading Japan will cost millions of lives. The new bomb will give the Japanese a way to surrender without losing honour. It will do horrible damage, but in the end it will save more people than it kills.

On July 26th, Japan rejected an Allied ultimatum to surrender. Truman decided to use the bomb. On August 6th, a B-29 dropped an atomic bomb on the Japanese city of Hiroshima.

The blast wiped out two-thirds of the city and killed nearly one hundred thousand people. Japan still refused to surrender. On August 9th, a second atomic bomb was dropped on Nagasaki.

Japan agreed to unconditional surrender. On September 2nd, 1945, Allied and Japanese military leaders boarded the American battleship "Missouri", anchored in Tokyo Bay. MacArthur spoke for the Allies.

"It is my earnest hope that from this solemn occasion a better world shall emerge out of the blood and carnage of the past."

The surrender was signed. World War II was over.

CRIMES AGAINST HUMANITY

At the end of World War II, for the first time in history, leaders of the defeated nations were made to stand trial for starting wars of conquest. Trials of twenty-eight Japanese leaders, held in Tokyo, condemned seven men, including Premier Hideki Tojo, to death by hanging.

On November 20th, 1945, war crime trials were held at Nuremberg, Germany. The four judges and four prosecutors represented Great Britain, the United States, the Soviet Union and France.

Twenty-one political and military Nazi leaders sat in the prisoners' dock.

The prosecution indicted the Nazis on four counts, one of which was crimes against humanity.

These crimes include murder, deportation of slave labour, ill treatment of prisoners, plunder and wanton destruction of cities, towns and villages. To say these men are not guilty would be to say there was no war.

The trials lasted for nearly one year. The prisoners were confronted with evidence of Nazi brutality.

Two million civilians were deported to Germany as slave labourers.

Thousands of documents and exhibits gave proof of Nazi crimes.

More than six million Jews were killed in Nazi death camps. Many underwent horrible tortures.

The most important Nazi tried was Hermann Goering, air force commander and originator of the concentration camps.

I had no idea such terrible things took place.

The judges listened and gave their verdict.

War crimes were committed on a vast scale never before seen in the history of war. They were for the most part the result of cold and criminal calculation.

THE COURT SENTENCED EACH PRISONER INDIVIDUALLY. THE FIRST WAS GOERING.

"HIS GUILT IS UNIQUE IN ITS ENORMITY. THE RECORD DISCLOSES NO EXCUSE FOR THIS MAN. VERDICT: GUILTY ON ALL FOUR COUNTS. SENTENCE: DEATH BY HANGING."

TEN OF THE OTHERS WERE ALSO SENTENCED TO BE HANGED. THREE WERE SENT TO PRISON FOR LIFE, AND FOUR RECEIVED FROM TEN TO TWENTY YEARS IN PRISON. THREE WERE ACQUITTED. ON OCTOBER 16TH, 1946, GUARDS CAME TO TAKE GOERING TO THE GALLOWS.

"HE'S POISONED HIMSELF. HE'S DEAD."

ONE BY ONE, THE OTHER TEN PRISONERS WERE LED TO THE SCAFFOLD.

TWELVE MORE TRIALS WERE HELD IN THE NEXT FEW YEARS. SOME TWO HUNDRED NAZI LEADERS WERE TRIED. THE FEW EXECUTIONS AND MANY PRISON TERMS COULD NEVER BRING BACK ANY OF THE MILLIONS OF NAZI VICTIMS. BUT THE WORLD COULD TAKE GRIM SATISFACTION THAT, FOR THE FIRST TIME, THE PLOTTERS OF WAR, PLUNDER AND MURDER HAD BEEN TRIED AND PUNISHED.

World War II: *Introduction*

by William B. Jones, Jr.

The names of heroes and villains continue to resonate more than seventy years later: Churchill; Hitler; Roosevelt; Stalin; Mussolini; De Gaulle; Tojo; Eisenhower; Rommel; Montgomery; Goering; Patton; Yamomoto; Nimitz; Himmler; Zhukhov; Goebbels; MacArthur; and so many more. The names of places associated with tragedy and triumph - with steadfastness and sacrifice - stretch out in a seemingly endless column: Warsaw; Dunkirk; Leningrad; Stalingrad; Lidice; Pearl Harbour; Bataan; Midway; Guadalcanal; Chelmno; Auschwitz; Treblinka; Buchenwald; El Alamein; Anzio; Monte Cassino; Kwajelein; Normandy; "the Bulge"; London; Dresden; Berlin; Manila; Okinawa; Iwo Jima; Hiroshima; Nagasaki; Nuremberg.

World War II was the defining event of the modern era. It killed and displaced millions of people. It altered political maps and the balance of power, creating superpowers and client states. Its ending advanced the fortunes of some and sent others to the gallows. Scientific advances were made, from the positive, such as the refinement of radar, to the destructive, such as Werner von Braun's V-2 rockets that rained death on London and other sites but that served as the basis for the postwar space program. A war begun with horses drawing German artillery and bearing Polish cavalry units ended with American atomic bombs vaporising two Japanese cities.

An ancient word, "Holocaust", acquired a new meaning; immediately upon the liberation of the Nazi death camps, it became the ultimate measure of evil. German philosopher Theodor Adorno famously asserted that "To write poetry after the Holocaust is barbaric." But humans make sense of experience, no matter how horrific, through the stories, songs, poems, and art we share. "For the dead and the living," Auschwitz and Buchenwald survivor Elie Wiesel declared, "we must bear witness." As the generations who lived that history as combatants or victims now pass away, those connected to them are charged with the responsibility not to forget.

As British historian Max Hastings wrote in *Inferno: The World at War, 1939-1945* (2011): "Within Western culture,...the conflict continues to exercise an extraordinary fascination for generations unborn when it took place. The obvious explanation is that this was the greatest and most terrible event in human history. Within the vast compass of the struggle, some individuals scaled summits of courage and nobility, while others plumbed the depths of evil, in a fashion that compels the awe of posterity" (Hastings 651). The Holocaust itself was unprecedented in scale in the annals of human depravity. Beyond it, the immeasurable suffering

London - St. Paul's Cathedral after the Blitz

Cont'd

inflicted on civilian populations around the world surpassed the worst excesses of any past conflagration. The unanswered questions of a Jewish woman at Auschwitz, addressed to a fellow prisoner who would within minutes carry her body to the crematorium, speak for millions: "I am still so young, I have really not experienced anything in my life, why should death of this kind fall to my lot? Why?" (Martin Gilbert, *The Second World War* [1989], p. 740.)

Warsaw, January 1945

From the atrocities in Poland that accompanied the German Blitzkrieg to the massacres that the Japanese perpetrated in China and the Philippines, the horrors of total war transcended all attempts to attach meaning. Still, civilisation demanded an accounting. War-crimes trials sought to establish a moral framework, while the work of witness was carried on through the efforts of such individuals as Nazi hunter Simon Wiesenthal, author Elie Wiesel (*Night*), US Marine veteran Eugene B. Sledge (*With the Old Breed at Peleliu and Okinawa*), filmmakers Claude Lanzmann (*Shoah*, 1985; *The Last of the Unjust*, 2013, among others) and Steven Spielberg (*Schindler's List*, 1993 and *Saving Private Ryan*, 1998), cartoonist Art Spiegelman (*Maus*), and many others. No act of justice or retribution could restore the lives lost or the wounds inflicted, but each retelling of the story, each approach to a different audience, constitutes the placement of a remembrance stone.

D-Day, 6th June 1944: US troops landing on Omaha Beach

This book, first published when the war was a mere two decades in the past, was and is a part of that effort.

∞

Fascinating Facts

Presented here are a selection of fascinating facts you may not know about World War II!

• At the conclusion of World War I, Germany was forced to sign the Treaty of Versailles. She lost all her overseas empires and also lost land to her neighbours. It restricted Germany from maintaining an army of more than 100,000 men. Most Germans opposed the Treaty, and their resentment would eventually undo the settlement, leading to World War II.

• Less than 3% of Germans voted for the Nazi party In the 1928 elections.

• Hitler was *Time* magazine's man of the year in 1938.

Cont'd

WORLD WAR II

- The swastika is an ancient religious symbol. It comes from the Sanskrit name for a hooked cross, which was a symbol of fertility and good fortune for ancient civilisations. It has been found in numerous ruins in Greece, Egypt, China, India, and Hindu temples.

- Neville Chamberlain's policy of appeasement towards Hitler in the years leading up to the outbreak of the war is generally thought to have been a mistake, but his defenders claimed that it bought Britain time to prepare for war.

- British engineer Robert Watson-Watt invented RADAR (**RA**dio **D**etection **A**nd **R**anging) while working on a "death-ray", intended to destroy enemy aircraft using radio waves.

- During air raids in Britain, barrage balloons were used to protect major towns and cities. The balloons had a network of steel cables beneath them, forcing bombers to fly high to avoid becoming tangled in the cables. This reduced their accuracy.

- The USA was the only nation that Germany formally declared war on. They did so on 11th December 1941.

- After the Japanese attack on Pearl Harbour, President Roosevelt wanted a bulletproof car. Due to budget constraints, however, the only available option was gangster Al Capone's personal limousine, which had been seized by the Treasury Department after he was arrested for tax evasion. Roosevelt told reporters, "I hope Mr Capone won't mind."

- The Siege of Leningrad killed more Russian people than all the American and British soldiers combined in the whole war.

- A US Navy recruit, Calvin Graham, was only 12 years old when he enlisted. He won a Bronze Star and a Purple Heart before his age was discovered.

- The blood transfusion saved countless lives during World War II and can be considered the most important medical advance of the time.

- Poison gas, first used in World War I, was only used by two nations in the Second World War: Japan (in China) and Italy (in Ethiopia in 1936).

- The Allies created a decoy invasion force to divert the German high command's attention from Normandy.

- Dummy paratroopers were dropped over different parts of Normandy to confuse the Germans. The decoy dummies exploded when they hit the ground.

- Paratroopers in Normandy carried a toy made by the ACME Whistle company which made the noise of a cricket to identify each other in the dead of night.

- On D-Day, John Steele, a US paratrooper, was left hanging *Cont'd*

USS *Arizona* after the attack at Pearl Harbour, 7th December 1941

The statue of John Steele hangs from the church steeple at Saint-Mère-Église

by his parachute which had become caught on the tower of the church in Sainte-Mère Église. He pretended to be dead for two hours while the fight went on below him. Today a parachute and a statue of Steele hangs from the same steeple.

• Anne Frank and her sister died at Bergen-Belsen concentration camp in March 1945, one month before the camp was liberated in April 1945.

• Winston Churchill lost the 1945 election immediately after winning World War II. He was later re-elected as Prime Minister in 1951.

• A nephew of Adolf Hitler, William Hitler, was in the US Navy during World War II. He changed his name after the war.

• Queen Elizabeth II served as a mechanic and driver during the war.

• Tokyo would have been the target had it been necessary to drop a third atomic bomb on Japan in August 1945.

• A Japanese soldier, Hiroo Onoda, never surrendered. For almost 30 years, until 1974 he held his position in the Philippines. His former commander travelled from Japan to personally issue orders relieving him from duty.

Discussion Topics

1) It can be argued that World War II was a "just" war, as it was fought to eliminate the tyranny of the Nazis and their totalitarian regime. Do you agree with this interpretation of the war? Do you feel that war can ever be "just"? Why? Why not?

2) Do you think Italy was unfairly represented in the peace treaties at the conclusion of World War I? Why?

3) Do you think the Japanese were justified in their invasion of Manchuria? In their attack on Pearl Harbour? Why? Why not?

4) "The Treaty of Versailles was the main cause of the Second World War." How far do you agree with this statement? Write an essay to explain why you agree/disagree. Include other causes and consider how important they might be in relation to the Treaty.

5) Write a diary entry as if you are a soldier in one of the following battles:

   a) The Battle of Britain
   b) The Siege of Stalingrad
   c) The Normandy Invasion
   d) The Battle of the Bulge

6) Do you think that the USA was justified in using the atomic bomb on Hiroshima and Nagasaki? Why? Why not? Do you agree that it was the sole reason that the Japanese surrendered?